Let's Talk About
ESTATE
PLANNING

Conversations about real-life
missteps in providing for loved ones
(and other things you didn't know about estate planning)

Let's Talk About
ESTATE
PLANNING

VIRGINIA A. McARTHUR, Esq.

Let's Talk About Estate Planning
Conversations about real-life missteps in providing for loved ones (and other things you didn't know about estate planning)

For information about this title or to order other books and/or electronic media, contact the publisher:

Cambridge Studio Publications
2425 L Street, NW
Suite 203
Washington, DC 20037
You can also order through
www.virginiamcarthur.com or Amazon.

ISBNs:
978-1-7343347-0-8 (Print)
978-1-7343347-1-5 (eBook)

Printed in the United States of America

Cover and Interior design: 1106 Design

For Michael, who is everything.

CONTENTS

PREFACE   ix

ACKNOWLEDGMENTS   xv

GLOSSARY   xvii

PART ONE
Elements of the Estate Plan

CHAPTER ONE   *Wills and Probate*   3

CHAPTER TWO   *Testamentary Trusts*   43

CHAPTER THREE   *Joint Ownership and Similar Arrangements*   59

CHAPTER FOUR   *Beneficiary Designations*   75

CHAPTER FIVE   *Revocable Trusts*   85

PART TWO
Other Planning Arrangements

CHAPTER SIX   *Gifts*   107

CHAPTER SEVEN   *Marital Rights*   115

CHAPTER EIGHT   *Assets for Minors and Other Young Folk*   133

CHAPTER NINE   *Charity*   153

PART THREE
Ancillary Documents

CHAPTER TEN   *Financial Powers of Attorney*   163

CHAPTER ELEVEN   *Documents Pertaining to Health Care Decisions*   173

PART FOUR
Important Miscellany

CHAPTER TWELVE   *Fiduciaries and Caregivers*   181

CHAPTER THIRTEEN   *Special Assets: Tangible Personal Property, Pets, Life Insurance, Digital Assets*   201

PART FIVE
Pulling It All Together

CHAPTER FOURTEEN   *Getting the Picture*   207

CHAPTER FIFTEEN   *Do I Have a Problem? What Should I Do?*   215

CHAPTER SIXTEEN   *Final Note*   227

APPENDIX A   *Helpful Websites*   229

APPENDIX B   *Information to Compile for Loved Ones*   235

ABOUT THE AUTHOR   241

PREFACE

The goal of this book is to help you keep the wrong people from inheriting your assets.

WHY THIS BOOK?

During the 35 years I practiced estate planning law, I spent many hours with clients explaining state and federal law, Probate, Wills, taxes, contracts, beneficiary designations, Trusts, various forms of ownership, and how these together formed the clients' estate plans.

Clients could rarely absorb all this important but unfamiliar information after one or two meetings. (This is a fact that many lawyers do not recognize!) The clients might walk out of the office semi-understanding the plan and later realize, perhaps with some chagrin, that they were not quite clear about the function of the elements and how they worked together. Out of embarrassment or fear of increasing their legal fees, they might hesitate to ask follow-up questions.

A client who is foggy on the function of the components of the estate plan and unwilling to ask follow-up questions is vulnerable to being swayed by friends and other influences. Such a client might exercise self-help—creating joint accounts, giving assets to minors, or rewriting documents. In doing so, a client can disinherit a loved one, skew the distribution of the estate, create a tax burden, or make the process of settling the estate needlessly complicated (and much more expensive).

Or, a client can achieve these results by following bad advice. Bad advice is advice that does not fit *your* assets and *your* wishes. Note: advice that is bad for *you* may be good for *others*. Advice, even from financial professionals like brokers, insurance advisers, or financial planners, can be good or bad, depending on your assets and your wishes. If the advice changes the disposition of your assets, you should have your estate planning attorney evaluate it in the context of your full estate plan. Reading this book will sensitize you to advice that can affect the disposition of your assets.

Some folks just don't review their plans when they should. When a friend of mine died a few years ago, his daughter learned to her dismay that her apartment, which he had intended to give her, was not really hers because his name was still on the documents. The stepmother was claiming a big share and sued to get it. My friend, even when he knew he was dying, had not reviewed and corrected his plan.

I was bemoaning this situation to my friend Caitlin Evans, when she suggested that stories like his and other estate planning errors might make a book. I jumped at the idea. Such a book, I thought, could clarify estate planning for people who are smart and interested but not fully conversant with the elements of estate planning and how they fit together, and who have enough money to want to control who would get it, but not enough to obsess about tax consequences.

WHAT THIS BOOK IS AND IS NOT:

This book presents estate planning principles through fictional conversations about real problems, to show in a memorable and, I hope, clear, way how the parts of the estate plan work individually and together. Other books explain. This book attempts to illustrate.

Many of the invented conversations in this book occur in the office of Rebecca Dalton, a (fictional) lawyer specializing in Estates and Trusts law (often called "T&E," as that is easier to say than "E&T"). She took over the law practice of Ben Morgan when he retired. Some conversations are between Ben and his walking buddy, Roger Bailey. And some of the conversations are among friends, discussing what they have learned from one sad error or another.

Estate planning attorneys try to help clients leave their assets a) to whom they want, b) with appropriate people in charge, when the beneficiary is unable to manage money (and for other reasons), and c) to keep taxes at a minimum. This book focuses on the first two concerns.

This book is not about *estate tax* planning. As of 2020, the federal estate tax is imposed only when the taxable estate (plus lifetime taxable gifts) exceeds $11,580,000 (or, if the right steps are followed, a combined $23,160,000 for a married couple). This number is indexed for inflation and increases annually.

(For persons dying after 2025, this exemption will drop to $5 million per person, indexed for inflation.)

Hundreds of sources exist on planning to minimize estate taxes and other transfer taxes, but the subject matter is of greatest interest to advisers for that limited group of people wealthy enough to worry about the federal estate tax. This book may also be useful to people with assets in that range, but one hopes they have attorneys and accountants to help them with federal estate, gift, and generation-skipping transfer tax planning.

That being said, certain taxes are of interest to any client, and, in two sections of this book, you will find conversations involving income tax and capital gains tax. These types of taxes are incurred by many more of us than will ever have to worry about the federal estate, gift, or generation-skipping transfer tax.

There are also some non-tax issues you will not find discussed in this book. Among these are the issues involved in planning for small businesses, for special-needs beneficiaries, for assets in foreign countries, for firearms, and for management of the family vacation home. Although these issues are not rare, they are also not for everyone, and the considerations in dealing with them are more particular than I could cover in this volume.

This book does not discuss electronic Wills, which as of February 2020, were accepted in Arizona, Florida, Indiana, and Nevada. Since, then, because of the pandemic, among other reasons, other states are adopting e-Will statutes. It is the nature of estate planning law that changes will continue to occur as the world around us changes.

This book is written primarily for persons domiciled in "common law" property states. Estate planners use this term to distinguish most of the U.S. from the "community property" states of Arizona, California, Idaho, Louisiana, Nevada, New Mexico, Texas, Wisconsin, and Washington (and Alaska, if opted into). This book will apply to unmarried individuals in those states. I have touched on the effects of community property laws on rights of married persons in these states but have not discussed these effects exhaustively.

Finally, this book is not intended to give legal advice; state laws governing estate planning vary so much that, even were I to have that goal, I could not achieve it. And, as you will see in the following conversations, the applicability of any advice depends on the assets and goals of the client. My fervent hope is that this book will help the reader understand his or her estate plan and be an active partner in maintaining it, to ensure that the reader's assets flow to the intended beneficiaries, with the proper management, when death steps in.

HOW TO READ THIS BOOK:

One need not read this book in any particular order. The Glossary is presented at the beginning to make the meaning of an unfamiliar term easy to find. It makes slow reading. I **suggest that you skim the Glossary and then dive into the conversations in Chapters One through Twelve.** Chapter Thirteen discusses some common assets that require special attention. Chapter Fourteen may help you manage your lawyer. Chapter Fifteen helps pull together the lessons of the book and puts you on top of your estate plan. Chapter Sixteen is a final comment.

ONE MORE NOTE BEFORE YOU START:

The text of this book was complete before the World Health Organization declared the 2020 health crisis to be a global pandemic. In response to the need to maintain social distancing, numerous states have adopted or are in the process of adopting permanent or temporary changes to the rules pertaining to witnesses and notaries being in the same room. These law changes are not reflected in this volume.

ACKNOWLEDGMENTS

Writing this book has been fun. It has been a kick to illustrate the horrors of estate planning gone wrong—Abby learning that she has really given away part of her condo; Kathy learning that her late husband's gift of insurance to their children will lead to years of Court reporting; Denny Doolan's loved ones learning that half his estate will go to people he despised. I hope these characters will be real to the reader and their situations memorable, so the reader will not make the mistakes the characters (or their family members) have made.

I thank Caitlin Evans for starting me on this book and Alexandra Armstrong, whose guidance helped me get this book out the door. Between these two events, I had reviewers:

The lay reviewers who read and commented on all or parts of my manuscript—Dan Anderson, Pamelia Caswell, Terry Condon, Michael Higgins, Sandy Hannum, Jane Rice, and Donna Vidaurrazaga—gave me very helpful feedback on how these stories affected them, as sample members of the target audience. I am gratified that they would take the time to look at and comment on my book.

And I had legal reviewers: Leslie Smith, Esq. reviewed the manuscript and kept me on the right path in many regards. Professor John Price, of Seattle, Washington, who has never even met me, generously commented on the full manuscript and gave me language for community property points. Michelle Evans, Esq. made a thorough review of a late version of the manuscript, correcting and supplementing. I am profoundly grateful to all of them. Howard Zaritsky, Esq., a leader in estate planning law and a really nice guy, also gave me reassuring encouragement. Estate planning lawyers are a special breed.

The most consistent encouragement came from my very supportive and wonderful husband, Michael Higgins. He got me going again several times when I started to drag my feet.

I hope that any errors still remaining are minor, but, big or little, they are all mine.

~ GINNY MCARTHUR
   March 2020

Before we start . . . you might wish to skim this

GLOSSARY

THE LANGUAGE OF ESTATE PLANNING

Many of the terms used in estate planning do not arise in everyday conversation. In order to make them easy to find when they come up in the conversations that follow, they are listed below in alphabetical order.

What is an **ADVANCE MEDICAL DIRECTIVE (AMD)**? An advance medical directive, or AMD, is a document in which you give instructions for the extent and types of medical attention you want in the event you are unable to speak for yourself. Such a document names a proxy (an agent, usually a close family member or friend) to speak for you. In addition to naming a proxy, the AMD also often incorporates the language of a Living Will (described below).

What is the **ANNUAL EXCLUSION**? The annual exclusion is the combined value of gifts a person can make to someone other than a spouse or charity in a year before the donor incurs a legal obligation to file a gift tax return. Thus, it is a gift tax concept that arises in this book only because it is not uncommon for parents to make large gifts to children to reduce the amount of their estates going through Probate.

What are **ASSETS?** Assets are everything you own that has a financial value. These include bank and brokerage accounts, your house and other real estate, your retirement plans and IRAs, annuities, insurance, and "stuff" (cars, furniture, artwork, jewelry, that horrid lamp you got from Aunt Millie). "Assets" also include partnership interests, leases, frequent flyer miles, goodwill in a business, intellectual property rights, royalties, and more. If someone might want to buy it from you, it's an asset.

What is **BASIS?** Basis, or tax basis, is a figure used to calculate your gain (or loss) upon sale of an asset. Example: Allyson buys a house for $100,000, all cash. She adds a couple of rooms, some landscaping, and appliances that will convey with the property. These items cost her $40,000 and are added to her basis. She sells for $200,000. Her gain is $60,000, the excess of sale price over basis. Any capital gains tax would be due only on the $60,000; the remaining amount paid by the buyer is "return of basis."

Who are **BENEFICIARIES?** Your beneficiaries are the parties who will benefit from the assets you leave behind when you die. These may be humans, charities, or other entities, such as Trusts. For the most part, you are free to name any beneficiaries, and you are free to exclude persons who might expect to be beneficiaries. An exception is that a spouse has special rights protected by law. (Rights of former spouses are negotiated during the divorce.)

What are **BENEFICIARY DESIGNATIONS?** Beneficiary designations are forms completed for insurance companies, Trustees or custodians of IRAs, and Trustees of other types of retirement plans. The "owner"—this is the insured, the annuitant, the person earning the money—names a beneficiary to receive the insurance death benefit, or the annuity, or the retirement benefit when the owner dies. The beneficiary designation represents an agreement to let the financial institution manage assets (and be compensated) in exchange for the institution's promise to distribute the assets during life (to the owner) or at death (to the named beneficiary).

What is a **CODICIL?** A Codicil is a written amendment to a Will leaving in place all the provisions of the original Will except those changed by the Codicil. Where there is a Will and a Codicil, the two documents are considered together as a single document. A Will may have any number of Codicils, and all are considered together with the Will as a single document.

What is the significance of being in a **COMMON LAW** state? In common law states (all those except the community property states named below), a) there is no presumption that a spouse has an ownership interest in earnings of the other spouse, b) titling of assets is generally conclusive as to ownership, and c) the tax effect of acquiring a new tax basis at the death of one spouse applies only to the property owned by that spouse and (assuming U.S.-citizen spouses) one-half of assets owned with the surviving spouse.

What is **COMMUNITY PROPERTY?** The "community property" states (Arizona, California, Idaho, Louisiana,

Nevada, New Mexico, Texas, Washington, and Wisconsin) treat ownership and rights in property of spouses differently than these are treated in the "common law" states (all other states, except Alaska, which allows a couple to opt in or out of community property status). "Community property" refers to assets in which each spouse has an equal, undivided interest.

Married individuals in community property states may own separate property ("individual property" under Wisconsin law) *and* community property. "Separate property" is property owned by a spouse prior to marriage and (in most community property states) all property acquired after marriage by gift, inheritance, devise, or bequest. All other property acquired by either party during marriage is community property.

In the absence of a contrary agreement, during marriage, the earnings of each spouse become their community property. Under the law of some community property states, the income from separate property is separate property, and in others, it is considered to be community property. Each spouse owns an equal, undivided half-interest in all community property over which he or she has the power of testamentary disposition. However, some states limit the power of a spouse to make a unilateral gift of community property.

The concept is important in divorce, a subject not covered in this book, and also at death. Significantly, and beneficially, in community property states, when one spouse dies, the tax basis of the entire "community" is adjusted to date of death value. (Of course, if the value has gone down, this is not a great benefit.)

In community property states, legal ownership of a married person's assets is not conclusively determined by which spouse is named as owner on the asset's title or registration.

What are **DEATH TAXES?** The term "death taxes" is an informal and somewhat pejorative way to refer to taxes incurred *solely* by reason of a person's death. These include inheritance tax, estate tax, and generation-skipping transfer tax. Another form of transfer tax is gift tax, which, along with generation-skipping transfer tax, affects the imposition of estate tax when a person dies. Gift tax and estate tax have exemptions and exclusions that remove these taxes from concern for most Americans. "Death taxes" have a complicated relationship with the more familiar *income* tax system.

What is a **DECEDENT?** A decedent is you, when you die. You may die without a valid Will, making you an **INTESTATE DECEDENT**, or you may have a Will, in which case you are said to die "**TESTATE.**"

What are **DESCENDANTS?** Descendants are children, their children, and so on. In most states, adopted descendants are included in the term "descendants" without additional confirmation. In the field of estate planning, the term "issue" is sometimes used to refer to descendants.

What is **DOMICILE?** The concept of domicile is important because it defines where a decedent's estate is to be administered and, thus, what state's law controls. The concept involves determining where one intends to remain permanently, which is simple for persons who clearly live in only one place. But where is a person domiciled if he lives in several of his homes

LET'S TALK ABOUT ESTATE PLANNING

every year? Or if he dies in transition, leaving Maryland with the intention of moving permanently to Florida? Settling these issues may require Court action.

What is the **ELECTIVE SHARE?** The elective share is the amount of a decedent's estate that a surviving spouse is *entitled* to have, upon electing to take it *in lieu of* anything left to him or her in the Will. In community property states, there is no right to an elective share because the surviving spouse owns half of the community property anyway.

In common law property states, the method of rejecting the probate estate and electing to take the elective share is set by state law and must be complied with exactly for the election to be effective.

In some states, the elective share is calculated only with respect to the assets subject to Probate, ignoring assets owned jointly with others, gifts made by the decedent without the survivor's knowledge, retirement assets, and so on. In other states, the assets used for calculating the share are "augmented" so that the calculation may include all of the foregoing and more. The right to elect can be negotiated away in a prenuptial or postnuptial marital agreement.

What is **ESCHEAT?** "Escheat" is a rarely occurring phenomenon in which a government entity becomes the sole beneficiary of the Probate estate of a decedent who dies without a Will and without closely related family members, as defined in the applicable statutes. In more than 35 years of practice and hundreds of estate administrations, I had only one estate that escheated to the government. (It was in Washington, DC, where escheated funds are to be used for the poor.)

Another form of escheat not related to Trusts and estates is the takeover by a state government of accounts in banks, stock certificates, and other financial assets held by institutions that have lost contact with the owners. States maintain computer records of unclaimed property that one can search free of charge. The unclaimed property can be reclaimed by the owner or the owner's estate.

What is an **ESTATE PLAN?** An "estate plan" is a coordinated organization of all arrangements a person may have that manage and dispose of assets during a person's life and upon death. Thus, an estate plan includes a person's Will (with any Codicils to the Will), beneficiary designations, individual or joint ownership, powers of attorney for asset management, and Trusts. The disposition of assets may also be affected by creditors, marital agreements and other contracts, exercise of a power of appointment, and federal or state law. The estate plan also usually includes documents pertaining to health care and medical decisions.

What is **ESTATE TAX?** Estate tax is a *transfer tax* (we are most accustomed to dealing with *income tax*, a different thing altogether) imposed on transfers from the estate or control of a deceased person to his beneficiaries. The law provides many exemptions and exclusions, such as transfers to a charity or U.S.-citizen spouse. At the federal level, a 2020 decedent's estate must transfer more than $11,580,000 to beneficiaries other than a charity or a U.S.-citizen spouse before being required to pay federal estate tax. Lifetime taxable gifts affect calculation of the taxable estate, because the gift and estate tax are coordinated.

Many states impose a state estate tax. The value an estate must have before it is subjected to state estate tax may equal or be less than the federal value, depending on state law. Some states impose no state estate tax. The imposition and avoidance of these federal and state taxes are beyond the scope of this book.

What is an **EXECUTOR** or **EXECUTRIX**? See "Personal Representative."

What is **GENERATION-SKIPPING TRANSFER TAX**? The generation-skipping transfer tax is imposed on large transfers of wealth to a member of a generation when one or more intervening generations is still living. The taxable transfer may be made at death or as a gift, during life. The imposition and avoidance of this tax are beyond the scope of this book.

What is **GIFT TAX**? Gift tax is a tax imposed on a donor who transfers assets without compensation. There are numerous exceptions: gifts to charity, gifts to an individual aggregating annually to less than the annual exclusion (currently $15,000), payments to institutions for education, or to medical-care providers for care, and gifts to a U.S.-citizen spouse. Many gifts that do not incur tax are nevertheless reportable on a gift tax return, which is probably the most not-filed-when-due tax return the I.R.S. has ever produced. State level: Only one state levies a state gift tax: Connecticut. The imposition and avoidance of gift tax are beyond the scope of this book.

What is a **GRANTOR?** The person who establishes a Trust is often called a Grantor. That person may also be called a "**SETTLOR**," a "**TRUSTMAKER**," or a "**TRUSTOR**." These labels apply only to persons establishing a Trust while living, inasmuch as a testamentary Trust is established by the person writing the Will, who is known as the testator or testatrix.

Who are **HEIRS AT LAW?** Heirs at law (also called simply "heirs") are persons who survive a decedent and are related to the decedent as described in state law. In most states, heirs of any decedent, testate or intestate, are entitled to be given notice of a Probate proceeding for the decedent.

What is **INHERITANCE TAX?** A few states impose an "inheritance tax" on the *receipt* of assets from a decedent's estate. This tax is distinct from and in addition to the estate tax, which is a tax on the *transfer* of assets. Inheritance tax is payable by the recipient, whereas the estate tax is payable by the estate. Very few states now impose an inheritance tax, and those that do have exemptions for charity, certain family members, and small amounts.

What does it mean if someone dies **INTESTATE?** A person dying without a valid Will is said to have died "intestate." The Personal Representative of an intestate decedent pays administration expenses, taxes, and legitimate creditors, and distributes the remaining Probate assets to the decedent's heirs at law.

What are **ISSUE?** "Issue" are the same as descendants.

What is **JOINT PROPERTY?** Joint property is one way two or more people can own an asset together. The term "joint property" is usually used in reference to assets that will pass to the remaining owner or owners when one owner dies, or, since no documentation is involved to "pass" the asset, you could say that the interest of the remaining owners expands to include the decedent's interest.

Please note: Under the law in many states, in order for a "joint" asset to move to the other owner or owners at the death of one owner, the ownership must be described as "joint with right of survivorship" or "JWROS." In these states, failure of the title to spell out the right of survivorship may mean that, even if the term "joint" is used, the owners own the property as tenants in common. (See definition below.)

What is a **LIFE ESTATE?** A life estate is a right in (usually) real property that arises by operation of law or by gift and allows the spouse or other donee to occupy or receive the rents from the property for life, with ownership at the life tenant's death reverting to other owners. Life estates raise complicated questions, such as who is responsible for insuring and maintaining the property, making major repairs, and paying the real estate taxes. It is usually assumed that the life tenant will pay for current operating expenses. Life estates are inconvenient devices to accomplish goals that can be better accomplished by other means.

What is a **LIFE SETTLEMENT?** A life settlement is an arrangement whereby an insured sells a life insurance policy he has on his own life in exchange for cash while the insured is still living. The buyer continues to own the policy and then collects the insurance proceeds when the insured dies. For many years, these arrangements were not legally permissible because of fears that they would lead to premature and unnatural deaths (read, "murders").

What is a **LIVING WILL**? A Living Will does not dispose of assets. A Living Will is a document stating, in language found in state statutes, an individual's choice not to have extraordinary medical care in event of terminal illness, under the described circumstances. The document legally protects a doctor who, under the specified circumstances, does not take extraordinary efforts to maintain a person who has expressed a preference to be allowed to die. The Living Will language is often incorporated in an advance medical directive, as part of that document.

What is a **LIVING TRUST**? See Revocable Trust, below.

What is **MOLST**? See POLST, below.

What does **PER STIRPES** (per STIR peez) mean? *Per stirpes* is a term found in Wills, Trusts and beneficiary designations as a shorthand reference to a distribution plan that many people with children want to put in place: "by branches." The exact method of distribution varies from state to state. Let's say that Testator (T) makes a Will leaving his estate to his descendants, *per stirpes*. T has three children, A, B, and C. A has no children. B has one child. C has four children.

When T dies, if A, B, and C all survive him, they share the estate equally, in thirds. If T dies predeceased by B, B's child takes B's share, and A and C get one-third each. If T dies predeceased by A, who has no children, B and C each get one-half. In some jurisdictions, if T dies after *all* of his children have died, the division is half to B's children and half to C's children; in other jurisdictions, the division starts at the next generation, so each of the five grandchildren would receive one-fifth.

What is a **PERSONAL REPRESENTATIVE?** The term "Personal Representative" is now used in most states to refer to the person ("person" here could be an entity, such as a bank's Trust department) appointed by a Court to administer the Probate estate. This person is nominated in the decedent's Will (or by statute if the decedent died with no Will) and confirmed by the Court as qualified to wind up the decedent's affairs. The old, but still valid, term is **EXECUTOR** (or if a woman, sometimes **EXECUTRIX**) for cases in which there is a Will. If the decedent had no Will, the person winding up the decedent's affairs used to be (and may in some states still be) called the **ADMINISTRATOR** (or, if a woman, **ADMINISTRATRIX**). The Personal Representative is often referred to as "**the PR.**" The PR manages the Probate estate and is distinct from a Trustee, who manages a Trust. There may be multiple Co-PRs serving together.

What is **POD?** What is **TOD?** Payable on Death (POD) (pronounced with the individual letters, not like the word "pod") and Transfer on Death (TOD) labels on bank (POD) or brokerage (TOD) accounts provide for direct transfer to the surviving POD or TOD beneficiary when the account owner dies. There is no trip through the Probate Court for these assets, although they may be available to pay creditors. About half of the states also have laws allowing Transfer on Death deeds for real property.

What is **POLST**? What is **MOLST**? A Physician Order for Life Sustaining Treatment or a Medical Order for Life Sustaining Treatment (also known by several other names) is an ancillary planning document, by which an already-ill individual sets forth his wishes regarding maintenance through extraordinary means. The document is signed by a doctor or other medically trained individual, who interviews the patient while the patient is still mentally capable. The document becomes a medical order and thus is more likely to be honored by emergency medical personnel than a mere medical power of attorney, in which the agent of the terminally ill patient on his behalf states the patient's wishes. For more information, see *www.polst.org/map*.

What is a **POWER OF APPOINTMENT**? A power of appointment is a power granted in a document, usually a Trust agreement, allowing someone (even someone other than the Trustee), to dispose of part of the assets held in the Trust at a stated time or event. Example: "When my daughter dies, I give her the power by her Will to divide and distribute the remaining assets of the Trust I have established for her among her cousins, in any proportions she might wish."

What is a **POWER OF ATTORNEY**? A power of attorney is a power given (usually in writing) by the "principal" to an "agent" to allow the agent to carry out certain responsibilities for the principal. It may be immediately effective, or "springing." A springing power is effective only upon occurrence of an event, most often a determination that the principal is no longer capable of managing his financial affairs. The power of attorney should always be "durable" so that it will continue to be effective ("endure") if/when the principal loses capacity. No POA remains effective after the death of the principal.

What is a **PR**? See Personal Representative, above.

What is **PROBATE**? Probate is the legal process by which a person, the **PR**, winds up the affairs of a decedent, under Court supervision. The amount of supervision and specific Court reporting requirements imposed vary widely from state to state, as does the cost of involving the Court and the length of time the process requires.

Please note: The duration of an estate administration will be extended in estates that have any of the following: illiquid assets, fighting beneficiaries, a large number of assets or of beneficiaries, ambiguous Will provisions, incompetent Personal Representatives or estate attorneys, numerous creditors, unco-operative Co-Personal Representatives, or lack of liquidity to carry out administration tasks.

What is the **PROBATE ESTATE**? The "Probate estate" is that part of a decedent's assets that is administered subject to the Court Probate process, under state law. The assets in the Probate estate are those owned solely by the decedent, including "tenancy in common" interests. (In some community property states, the deceased spouse's estate includes both halves of the community property.) However, despite the control the decedent had over them, the following are *not* Probate estate assets: insurance left directly to beneficiaries, retirement plans with living beneficiaries named to receive assets at the death of the decedent, assets with a joint owner who survives the decedent, assets with a "POD" (Payable on Death) or "TOD" (Transfer on Death) designation, and assets the decedent has transferred during life to a Revocable Trust.

What is **PROPERTY**? "Property" is a term that estate planning attorneys equate with "assets." It includes both "real property," which relates to land and interests in land, such as oil rights, and also "personal property," which can be either "tangible" (you can touch it) or "intangible" (such as financial assets or goodwill in a business).

What is the **RESIDUARY ESTATE**? "Residuary estate," or sometimes just "residue" is the part of a decedent's Probate estate that remains after bills, taxes, administration expenses, and bequests are paid. The beneficiary of this part of the estate is the "**RESIDUARY BENEFICIARY**."

What is a **REVERSE MORTGAGE**? A reverse mortgage is a loan against one's residence that reduces the equity in that home. Such a loan is generally available to persons older than 62 who have substantial equity and low debt, and who are able to protect the home by paying ongoing insurance, taxes, and any applicable homeowner fees. The reverse mortgage may be used in an estate plan to create liquidity for a homeowner.

What is a **REVOCABLE TRUST** (often called a "Living Trust")? A Revocable Trust is a form of Trust in which a person gives bare legal title of assets to a Trustee, while retaining beneficial ownership. The written Trust document provides for management of such assets until death and then further provides for distribution of those assets after death. A Revocable Trust is commonly in this format: X establishes the Trust for the benefit of X and Mrs. X, with X (yes, himself) as the Trustee. X writes the Trust document to name a successor Trustee, Y, to take over in the event of X's incapacity or death. The Trust document gives Y instructions for distributing the assets of the Trust when X has died. In community property states, it may be common for X and Mrs. X to have a joint Revocable Trust.

What is **STATE LAW**? The term "state law" is used often by estate planning attorneys because so much of the operation of T&E law is determined by specific state requirements. "State law" refers to the written statutes, regulations, and the decided cases of the state or other jurisdiction, such as the District of Columbia, in which the decedent's estate is to be administered. The primary jurisdiction of administration is the jurisdiction in which the decedent was domiciled at death. Ancillary Probate administration may be required in other jurisdictions where the decedent owned certain assets at death, such as interests in real property.

What are **TENANTS BY THE ENTIRETY**? Tenants by the entirety are spouses, in common law states. T by E ownership provides a right of survivorship between spouses. This form of ownership protects the assets from creditors of a single spouse.

What are **TENANTS IN COMMON**? Tenants in common are two or more owners of an asset who retain a separable interest in an asset they own together, with no right of survivorship. For example: May and her sister June own a beach house as tenants in common. When May dies, June does not inherit May's half of the beach house. May's interest in the beach house is, instead, an asset of May's Probate estate and passes to her beneficiaries under her Will. *Note*: When one leaves real property to more than one beneficiary, the beneficiaries usually take the property as tenants in common.

What does **TESTATE** mean? A person dying testate dies with a valid Will.

What is a **TESTAMENTARY TRUST?** A testamentary Trust is a Trust the terms of which are stated in a Will to take effect at the death of the testator.

What is a **TESTATOR** or **TESTATRIX?** This is the person who makes a Will. Some states distinguish gender, in which case "Testatrix" refers to a woman who makes a Will.

What is **TOD?** See **POD**, above.

What is a **TRUST?** A Trust is an arrangement by which a person gives assets to a Trustee to manage for the benefit of a beneficiary or beneficiaries. The Trust is almost always in writing. The kinds of Trusts that could be in an estate plan and the purposes for which they can be established are limited only by imagination, but the one constant is that there are three parts: (1) a Trustee, (2) assets, and (3) one or more beneficiaries.

The person who establishes the Trust may be called the "Settlor" or "Trustor" or "Grantor" or "Trustmaker," or if the Trust is established under a Will, that person is simply the testator. The person in charge of carrying out the terms of the written agreement is the "Trustee." The person who benefits from the arrangement is the "Beneficiary." There is no actual Trust until there are assets, sometimes called a "res" (thing), for the Trustee to manage. In law school, we learned that this "res" could be as minimal as "a peppercorn."

What is a **TRUSTEE**? A Trustee is the person, persons, or entity responsible for using assets of a Trust to carry out the intention of the Grantor of a Trust. In doing so, the Trustee must comply with the terms of the Trust, plus applicable state and federal law, and must exercise independent judgment in the investment and distribution of Trust assets. In some estate plans, there may be a **TRUST PROTECTOR**. Discussion of the Trust Protector concept is beyond the scope of this book.

What is **UTMA**? UTMA stands for **UNIFORM TRANSFERS TO MINORS ACT**. The law, some version of which has been adopted in all U.S. jurisdictions, provides a way for a minor to own assets while giving authority to an adult, the "custodian," to manage those assets for the benefit of the minor. UTMA replaced a prior law, the **UNIFORM GIFTS TO MINORS ACT**, which had more limitations on the kinds of gifts that could be made to minors under the law.

State law varies as to the age to which UTMA gifts may be held. In most states, a minor reaches majority at age 18, but many states allow UTMA gifts (either all of them or certain of them) to be managed to age 21, and some states allow UTMA accounts to continue to age 25. When the former minor reaches the age of termination of the UTMA account, the custodian is supposed to transfer the UTMA assets directly to the former minor.

What is a **WILL**? A Will, or Last Will and Testament (historically, the Will related to stuff and the Testament to real estate—a distinction no longer made in most states), is a written document in which an individual, the Testator, names a party (the "PR") to administer his Probate estate and distribute it to the named beneficiaries. If the written document does not comply with the requirements of state law, it will not be honored as a Will.

PART ONE

Elements of
the Estate Plan

CHAPTER
ONE

WILLS AND PROBATE

What goes into a Will? Can I write my own Will? Should I? Does having a Will keep my estate out of Probate? How bad is Probate, anyway? What happens if I die without a Will? What does a Will control?

BOB REVIEWS HIS FIRST WILL

Rebecca Dalton, Esq. has drafted a Will for Bob Schmidt. It is Bob's first Will, and he has questions about the draft Rebecca sent him, so he asks for a telephone meeting to go over the document.

"Hi, Bob. Thanks for calling. Where would you like to start?"

"Thanks, Rebecca. Well, first, you know I've never done a Will before. I want to be sure I can change it if I get married or whatever."

"Definitely. The Will is considered 'ambulatory.' Love that term, but it just means that you can change it until you can't—that is, until you either lose your mental ability or you

3

die. You'll probably have several Wills before you're done. And, of course, the Will is not effective until you die."

"OK, that's good. Now let's look at this. I understand starting the Will with my name and where I'm from, but why mention that I have no wife or children?"

"That is really just to reassure the Court that you are writing this Will not to omit any close family but because you don't have a wife or children yet."

"Well, I don't, but why mention that?"

"Because a wife or a child who existed but whom you omitted might have rights to some of your assets."

"I thought you could leave children out!" exclaimed Bob.

"You *can* omit children, but you have to admit that they exist to be sure that omission will be effective. You can't let the Court just think you forgot them."

"OK, well not an issue yet! Well, of course, I have my cat, Tammie. But I see where this draft Will gives Tammie to my friend Bonnie along with some money for Tammie's care."

Bob consulted the list of questions he had compiled. "Next, I see that you don't list my assets. You had me bring all those papers to you about my brokerage and bank accounts and my apartment, but you don't list them in the Will. Why not?"

Rebecca smiled. "This is a common question. I wanted to review your assets so I could be sure to advise you properly—it's my job to be sure we set up everything to accomplish your goals.

"The Will applies to everything you own in your individual name when you die. So, I wanted to see your account papers to make sure I knew whether your accounts were actually titled in your individual name. If you owned them jointly with someone else, or if you had put Payable on Death or Transfer on Death provisions on them, they would not go under the Will.

"I have had clients tell me how they owned assets and then found from the paperwork that they were mistaken. I like to see the actual paperwork to assure myself about this, because I want to be sure your documents suit your particular situation. The papers show that you own all of your assets individually."

"OK. Well, why doesn't my Will list my assets, then?"

Rebecca explained: "We don't need to list each asset in your Will because the assets you own at the time you eventually die will be identified then. This Will—or the most recent one you have made before you die—applies to whatever those assets are, even to an asset you, say, acquired the day you expired. Hey, that rhymes!"

"Cute. How does someone know what my assets are when I die? Do I have to keep a list somewhere?" asked Bob.

"Well, a list certainly can help your Personal Representative, that is, your brother Frank. It is up to Frank as your Personal Representative, or PR, to find out what you own when you die. He does this by looking at your financial records, your tax return, the files in your apartment. And, of course, I have a record of your assets as they are right now, so there's a point to start from.

"Your Will affects your individually owned assets, not joint accounts, not retirement accounts, and a couple of other exceptions. You might change brokers, you might open new bank accounts, you might acquire a boat, and so on. As long as you remain a resident of this state, you won't need to change your Will to reflect asset changes. Of course, getting married would require a change."

"Or moving, I gather."

"Yes, if you move out of state, you should have your Will reviewed to be sure it complies with the law of the new state. Even if a change is required, it's possible it could be done by Codicil. A 'Codicil' is an amendment to a Will," explained Rebecca. "State law is paramount in interpreting and carrying out the terms of Wills."

"So, here's a question," said Bob. "In this Will, I'm giving my motorcycle to Bill Phillips and my camera gear to Alicia Martin. What if I had a bunch of additional gifts I wanted to make, like these?" Bob asked.

"OK. Well, in an instance where you want to give a specific item to someone, you would list it in your Will. It's not uncommon to want to give a few things to friends or certain family members. Putting clear provisions in the Will ensures that they get those items—as long as you still own them when you die.

"If you have a lot of these gifts, you might want to make a separate list outside the Will. The Will could refer to this list and request your PR—that's Frank—to carry out your wishes, but this is less secure. Some states will honor this, but others might not.

"Keep in mind, though—every person you have listed in your Will to get something is entitled to a legal notice when you die. The more gifts, the more legal notices. These are not a hassle, really, but it's something to keep in mind if you think you will have a lot of these items. But I would never recommend that you use your Will to make a gift of a particular financial asset."

That surprised Bob. "You mean, if I wanted my friend Alicia to have $25,000, and I actually have an account of that size, I should *not* make a Will provision saying, 'I give my account at Really Large Savings Bank to my friend Alicia'?"

"Exactly right."

"Why not?" wondered Bob.

"Because it would be way too easy for you—and I don't mean just you, but anyone—in a few years to forget about this provision and move your account out of RLSB to some other bank or to use the account to buy something. Then Alicia is cut out, perhaps unintentionally. If you wanted Alicia to have $25,000, your Will would just say, 'I give my friend Alicia the sum of $25,000 if she survives me.'"

"But what if I don't have an asset when I die that equals that dollar amount? How does she get paid?" Bob was concerned.

"Well, try not to think about your financial assets as individual potatoes. Instead, think about a stew in a pot, adding together the values of all of your assets. Your Personal Representative will liquidate your assets and ladle out your beneficiaries' shares after providing for final taxes, expenses of handling the estate administration, and so on."

"So, I could even just put percentages in my Will? Right now, I'm just giving most of my stuff to Frank. At some point, I might want to add some beneficiaries," pointed out Bob.

"Sure. Right now, you have only a few beneficiaries named in your draft Will, and your brother Frank is the main one. He gets whatever is left after the gifts to your friends are made and the expenses are paid. That makes him your 'residuary beneficiary.' If you had a bigger bunch of beneficiaries, I would suggest making percentage bequests, to keep everyone proportional. Like, 'I give 25 percent of my estate to X, 15 percent to Y,' and so on. But you're not in that situation—you make a few specific gifts, and give the rest to your brother Frank."

"OK—this is good. I feel a lot more on top of this document than I did before this meeting! Thanks. I'll see you next Tuesday for the signing."

BOB COMES IN TO SIGN HIS WILL

"Hi, Rebecca. I thought I should mention one more thing that might affect my Will in the future," said Bob.

"Sure!" responded Rebecca. "What's on your mind?"

"I'm mentioning this in case you need to know about it. I might legally change my middle name from Zane to Horrock, my mother's maiden name. Does that do anything to this Will?"

"Yes, but it's minor. At the beginning of the Will, where we state your name as Robert Zane Schmidt, we would need to add 'also known as Robert Horrock Schmidt.' We list all names by which you have ever been known."

"Why not just my final correct name?" asked Bob.

"The reason for this is that, over a lifetime, you might acquire assets titled in slightly different versions of your name.

This happens with people who marry and change their names. And you have legal name-change situations. And sometimes people use a middle name and initialize their first name, or they become known by a nickname, and own something in that nickname. So, there are many ways someone could own assets in more than one name."

"Hmmm, I never thought about that calcifying of the nickname. That happens all the time!"

"Yup," Rebecca continued, "if all names in which you might own anything, including social security, old stock certificates, and the like, are listed in your Will, when the Will 'matures' (if you'll excuse an estate planning joke), your Personal Representative does not have to go back to Court to prove that Robert Zane Schmidt is the same person as Robert Horrock Schmidt. Putting all the names in the Will means that when the Court appoints the Personal Representative, that PR has authority to take control of assets you own in any and all of your various names."

"I see. So, if I do this name change, can I just write the other name into my Will when the Court procedure is done?"

"*Oh, no!* Please do not write on your Will at all after it's signed! *This is really important.* Changes written on your Will might invalidate the Will. And, of course, you would be dead when this came to light and unable to tell the Court what you wanted.

"Instead of writing your new name on your Will document, just call me up. I will draft a short Codicil. This is an amendment that becomes part of your Will—and you'll sign it with witnesses and all the formality we are using today as you sign this Will."

Bob commented, "OK, one thing you just said raises another question. You said something about the Court 'appointing' the Personal Representative. If the Court appoints the PR, why am I naming my brother in the Will to be the PR?"

"Ah, I see. Well, *you* nominate the PR, but the Court has to approve your choice for the selection to be effective. This is hardly ever a problem, but some people are not eligible. For example, if your brother were serving felony time at a federal prison at the time of your death, he would not be eligible. There are some other disqualifiers, but I asked you all of the relevant questions when you came in last week, and I have no doubt that your brother would be approved.

"However," Rebecca continued, "if you ever do move to a new state, you should have your Will checked by a lawyer in your new state. It's possible that the law of that state would not allow your brother to serve, or that there might be additional costs of having him serve.

"For example, some states have extra bonding requirements if the PR lives out of state. That can increase the expense of administering the estate. Some states allow a non-U.S. citizen to serve, but only if that person resides in the U.S. All of this varies by state law. It would be a lot easier if every state had the same law, but the true situation is far from that!"

"OK, so I get it: state law rules!"

"So true."

DENNY DOOLAN, ESQ.'S AMATEUR WILL

"Hello?"

"Hi. My name is Wendell McGraw. May I please speak with Margaret Doolan?"

"This is she," replied Margaret, thinking what a warm voice this Wendell McGraw had.

"Oh, hi. It's nice to talk with you. Someone had pointed you out to me at Denny's funeral, but I never got over to meet you."

"It was a nice, service, I thought. But so sad—I mean for him to die at age 42 of a heart attack—I haven't quite absorbed it yet."

"Yes, I feel the same way," said Wendell. "Well, if I might broach the subject of my call, I am sitting here with the Last Will and Testament of W. Denis Doolan, and I would like to get some help from you."

"Oh, sure. What is it you think I can do?" asked Margaret.

"Well, Denny named me to be Executor—I'm called the 'Personal Representative,'" he said, reading the unfamiliar designation off his paperwork. "Denny and I had become quite close in the last few years. We met during workouts at Jumbo's Gym and just hit it off, to the point that we would see each other about once a week for dinner. We even had keys to each other's apartments. When I heard that Denny had died, I went to his apartment to make sure the newspapers were not piling up, to water the plants, you know—make sure everything was secure.

"He had told me if anything ever happened to him to find his Will in his apartment. I thought I needed some guidance, so I called a friend of mine who is a Trusts and Estates lawyer, Rebecca Dalton. She told me that, since I am named as PR, I could remove the Will from the apartment, but nothing else."

Wendell continued: "Anyway, the thing is, I need to get some family information, and I thought you might be able to help. Incidentally, I should mention that Denny's Will made a bequest to you, and I have to say it's really nice. In his words, he makes the bequest, quote, 'To my former wife, Margaret Doolan, in gratitude for her continuing friendship and in awe of her fabulous sense of humor.'"

"Wow, that does sound nice! Sounds just like Denny. May I ask how much he left me?"

"Well, the bequest is for $50,000, Margaret."

"Fifty thousand dollars!??! Oh, gosh—I think I'm going to cry. Denny could be so sweet. The marriage didn't work out—ha, maybe we just needed a little more space in our togetherness—but he did have some fine points," Margaret reflected on her feelings for Denny.

Wendell went on: "The Will left the rest of his estate to set up a fund for the Boys and Girls Clubs of America. My guess is that he did that because it was a way to continue the family name, since he had no children. You know, his parents had died, and his brother had died—all very young. But I do have some questions about more remote family members, and I hope you can help, Margaret."

"OK. Well, fire away."

"The brother who died—did he have any children?"

"No."

"And were there any other siblings I might just not have heard of?"

"No, I'm quite sure of that."

"OK," said Wendell, "so Denny had no surviving parents, children, spouse, siblings, nieces, or nephews. What can you tell me about his parents' siblings?"

"Huh! That's a funny question. Well, his mother had a brother, George—I think he lives in Atlanta. I think his mother's maiden name was 'Brock.' Then, his father had a brother, too, also named 'George,' coincidentally. George Doolan died while Denny and I were still married. He had a couple of bratty kids—Larry and Jimmy, I think their names were."

Margaret went on: "Denny and I went to Uncle George's funeral. Denny was disgusted by the way his cousins were behaving. We heard they had already had a big fight with some other family about how expensive a casket they should get. There was a lot of gossip at the funeral about how, when their father was still alive, Larry and Jimmy had cut back the hours of the housekeeper/caretaker to save money, how they had taken their father's collection of fine watches out of the house, and how they had ransacked the place for financial information before their father died. It was appalling."

"Oh, dear," said Wendell. "Any idea where these cousins might live?"

"I think they're still in Scranton, Pennsylvania. May I ask why you need this information?"

"Sure. Well, first, let me mention that I am a lawyer, but not one in Trusts and Estates—I do environmental litigation."

"On the side of the angels, I hope?" confirmed Margaret.

"Oh, absolutely. Anyway, when I called this lawyer, Rebecca Dalton, she told me that I could take the Will from his apartment and that she would help me with the next steps."

"Is it going to be complicated?"

"Well, here's where it gets pretty weird. It seems that Denny had prepared his own Will. In a lot of places, it looked pretty good. I mean, it named an Executor, made the bequest to you and to the fund for the Boys and Girls Clubs, provided for payment of bills, and, in fact, even named a backup Executor for me," noted Wendell.

"I think I hear a 'But' coming."

"Right. After clearly thinking through all of his wishes and putting them down with care—like the bequest to you, made so thoughtfully—he had the Will notarized."

"So, that sounds good!" Margaret exclaimed.

"Yeah, it *sounds* good, but I have learned from Rebecca, it's not good enough. That is all he did. He signed the Will in front of a notary, who notarized the document."

"And . . . ?"

"Well, Rebecca told me, in practically every state in the country and the District of Columbia, you need at least two witnesses. In this state, two witnesses will be enough. But never one."

"You mean, even if it's notarized, you still need witnesses?"

"Yes. You don't even have to notarize it, really, for it to be valid in a lot of places, although Rebecca told me that, in some states, having the Will notarized can speed up getting the Court to accept the Will. But the one rock-bottom requirement is that you have to have two witnesses and, to be safe, she said, even three. The witnesses should be of age, but, here, that's just 18 nowadays, and they should not be related or have any interest in the Will or in the estate.

"And there are other requirements. The testator—that's the person signing the Will—has to sign first and, usually, in the presence of the witnesses, although in some states, the testator can show his signature to the witnesses and confirm that he signed it. The witnesses have to know they are witnessing a Will but not what is in it. And after the testator signs, the witnesses have to sign in the presence of each other. I'm sure there's some historical reason for this."

"Gee—who knew!"

"Well, apparently not Denny."

"Yes, I guess not. Well, what does that mean, anyway?"

"Well, it means that, in effect, Denny died without a Will."

"What?!? Can't you show this document to the Court and tell them you want to follow its directions?"

"I'm afraid not. Rebecca tells me that no, they won't do it. Never. Not at all. Period. Like, no chance."

"Never? There must be a lot of people who think notarizing is enough," commented Margaret. "Well, my $50,000 just went up in smoke, I guess. So, what happens to the money when someone dies without a Will?"

"Well, you could say that nobody really dies without a Will," noted Wendell.

"How do you mean?"

"In fact, in every state and in D.C., the legislature has set out in the laws of the state who gets your money if you die without a Will. It's like a Will written for people who don't get around to doing their own."

"Does the government get it? That's what I would guess."

"No, no—it's not that bad. Here in Maryland, if a person dies with no children, parents, or descendants of parents, you move up the line to grandparents. Denny didn't have a living grandparent, so we move down to descendants of grandparents."

"What do you mean, 'move'?"

"Well, I mean, the money settles where the moving finger stops. So, imagine a family tree. You move your finger up the tree to, in Denny's case, his grandparents. Then, since there are no living grandparents on either side, you move your finger down the line of descent from each set of grandparents until you find someone alive. At that point, the finger stops moving. And the money drops."

"Hmm. So, in Denny's case, his mother's parents' living descendant is his mom's brother George, and his father's parents' living descendants are those horrible cousins in Scranton?"

"Uh, yes. I'm afraid so. The Atlanta uncle gets half, and those undeserving little bums in Scranton will get the other half of Denny's estate. The Boys and Girls Clubs get nothing, and your bequest is just a gesture—not to mention, my appointment as Executor has no effect. I'm just getting this information so that Rebecca and I can notify the next of kin that they need to do something."

"Ugh. And today started so well. I'm just crushed that this is happening."

"I know. Listen, Margaret, I know this is forward, but I really appreciate what Denny had told me about you. Could I take you for lunch sometime? I can tell you some other stories Rebecca has told me about how people can mess up their Wills."

"Sure. That would be nice."

WENDELL AND MARGARET MEET FOR LUNCH

Margaret Doolan and Wendell McGraw meet for lunch the following Saturday at a quiet place in Arlington, Virginia. They have come to know each other a bit over the meal, including finding out that they both have blocs of tickets to Washington Nationals baseball games.

Over coffee, Margaret reminds Wendell: "I think you told me you had some stories from your lawyer friend Rebecca about how people mess up their Wills. I'm still not over the horrible reality that Denny's money is going to people he despised. It just seems so wrong. But what are some of the other stories?" Margaret asked.

"Oh, right. Well, first Rebecca told me that it is perfectly legal for a person to write his own Will—it's not a crime, or anything. It's just usually a bad idea because people can make such innocent mistakes with such dire consequences. Like Denny thinking that having his wishes notarized would suffice. You can get a form—they used to sell them at stationery stores, but now you can get them from companies like Legal Zoom. The forms are fine, but you have to understand how they fit in with your assets, and you have to complete them correctly."

"There's a wrong way to complete a form Will?"

"Oh, yes. Rebecca said one of the worst screwed-up Will cases she ever saw involved a woman who had used a form Will. The woman had wanted just two of her four children to have her estate. I gather two of them had been completely out of touch and mean to her, so she was just leaving her estate to the others.

"In this case, it didn't matter what the woman wrote in the Will, because one of her sons took the Will form to church to have a couple of people witness it, and when it was done, he brought it back home for his mother to sign. Needless to say, when the facts came out, the Court determined that she died without a Will. The witnesses have to sign *after* the person making the Will, they have to know they are witnessing a Will, and they have to watch each other sign. Rebecca said that, as a result of that failed Will, the four children shared equally, as the woman's heirs."

"Well, a windfall to the two others, then," Margaret exclaimed.

"Right! Then, someone else Rebecca knew made a gift to a friend in the Will, $20,000, and then had the friend be one of her two witnesses to the Will, which invalidated the gift!"

"You mean being a witness might disinherit you?"

"Yup. If there had been a third witness, it would have been OK, because two witnesses are enough, and they could just ignore the one who got the bequest. And, of course, if the witness would inherit anyway without a Will, the invalidating of the bequest might not matter.

"Then there was a case where a physicist—I mean, a really educated guy!—helped his dying friend write her Will. She was one of those people who like animals more than people—she made a bequest to a family of raccoons. Rebecca said this could work if a Trust were established in the Will, with instructions on how to care for them, but the physicist had not written a Trust into the Will (Who would, other than a professional, really?), and when the lady died, a lot of Court time—and legal expense—was involved in making the woman's wishes happen."

"Wow! The things people want to do with their money!" exclaimed Margaret.

"I know. And they can do a lot of what they want legally—they just have to do it the right way, or the law won't recognize it. And straightening it out—when the person who knew what she wanted is dead and can't explain it—well, that can take a lot of time and huge legal expense.

"Another kind of surprising thing Rebecca told me is that these legal problems are not confined to nonlawyers writing their Wills. Rebecca said she has had several Probate matters of deceased lawyers who wrote their own Wills, as Denny did. In *every single one* of them there was some small thing that, if done differently, would have made the estate administration simpler or cheaper."

Margaret was incredulous. "Every single one? Is the Court just looking for something to shoot down?"

Wendell confirmed: "Yes, as to every single one, and, no, I don't think the Court was trying to make things difficult. These were lawyers practicing in fields other than Trusts and Estates. A typical one, she told me, was a case where the Will had the necessary two witnesses, and everything looked good, but the attestation language was missing. That's the language at the end of a Will right before where the witnesses sign. The language says something like, 'Yes, indeed, we, the witnesses, did see the testator sign the Will, and we then watched each other sign the Will as witnesses, and we did it all on the 10th day of June 2012,' or whatever.

"As you can see—if you have that language, right there on the face of the document there is evidence that all the proper procedures were followed when the Will was signed. In Maryland and DC, that tells the Court what it needs to know about the circumstances of signing. Rebecca told me that, in Virginia, the Wills have that language and double up by having a notary page re-confirming the whole thing, with additional signatures. But this lawyer's Will that I'm talking about didn't have the one or two sentences spelling all of that out."

"So, what happened when he died?"

"Well, it wasn't terrible, but it was extra work—that means extra expense paid by the estate to the lawyer. Before the Will could be accepted for Probate, Rebecca had to get sworn testimony from the two witnesses—fortunately, she was able to locate them—that yes, it had happened the way it was supposed to, all spelled out.

"Now, if she had been able to find only one of those witnesses, I don't know what would have happened—I don't know if the sworn testimony of the one would be enough to swear to the presence of the other. But in Rebecca's case, that avenue did not have to be explored. And if she hadn't been able to find either of them, I wonder if there would have been an intestacy. Imagine the whole Will being invalid for the lack of two sentences. Believe me, hearing these stories, even though I have practiced law for 20 years, I would not write my own Will."

"Hmm. Food for thought. I'm trying to remember when I last looked at my Will!"

Wendell continued: "In a more surprising case, Rebecca told me she once handled a judge's estate. This man had actually practiced Trusts and Estates law out west, in a different state, but he died a resident of Virginia after moving East, because he had been appointed to a federal judgeship in DC. Rebecca said his Will was complete, with all the language you need for attestation, and so on. The Will provided a Trust for the judge's wife, who did survive him, and so on—all thought out."

"So, what was the problem, then?"

"Well, in Virginia, if you have a Trust within a Will, like the Trust the judge put into his Will for the benefit of his wife, such a 'testamentary' Trust has to file annual accountings with the Commissioner of Accounts for the county of domicile.

"This accounting is a kind of onerous thing to put together, at least the first couple of times until you get the hang of it. It accounts for all transactions in the Trust during the year since the last account, states the current assets, and so on, under oath. It has to balance to the penny. You have to follow the prescribed format, and the account is reviewed by the Commissioner of Accounts. Sometimes the Commissioner asks for additional paperwork to complete the review. You might have to pay someone to assemble this accounting, and you have to pay the Commissioner for reviewing it. So, kind of a hassle and an expense," Wendell commented.

"But the thing is, some time ago, but in Rebecca's memory, the Virginia General Assembly modified the account-filing requirement. The new law said that, if the Will contains a sentence waiving the accounting requirement, it is not necessary for the Trustee to file these annual accounts. You still account to the beneficiaries, but you don't have to have the Commissioner review everything."

"So, I'm guessing the judge's Will didn't waive the filing of accounts?"

"Correct. One sentence more in the otherwise perfect Will would have saved the judge's family a lot of aggravation and quite a bit of expense in preparation fees, plus the annual fees to the Commissioner's Office for reviewing the accounts. One measly sentence."

"Wow."

"Yup. Rebecca said that, if the judge had lived in DC or Maryland, there would have been no issue, because they don't have that accounting requirement. But Virginia law is different. That's one thing that can make T&E so tricky—it is very state-specific. Not just about Trusts in Wills, but in many, many ways.

"If I might change the topic," noted Wendell, "the Nats game at Philadelphia is just about to start. Want to go to Scoop's for a beer and watch the game?"

"Sure! That sounds great."

THE DISASTROUS PERFECT WILL

"Hey, Frenchy—it's Murph. Can you get out of work and meet me at Scoop's at 6 o'clock?"

"Sure, what's up?"

"I just need to talk. I'm paying."

"Well, OK, then. See you at six."

Adrienne Murphy and Camille French never had trouble finding a seat at Scoop's at six, and tonight was no exception. They got a booth, ordered their craft beers, and got some peanuts.

Camille asked, "You sound a little frazzled—what's going on?"

"Well, it's about Colleen's Will. You remember that my friend Colleen O'Brien died a couple of months ago? I can't remember—did you ever meet her?"

"I think once, just before I moved away, but by the time I got back here, she was in a retirement community, and I never saw her again."

"OK. Well, Colleen had been in the Foreign Service. A short early marriage, no kids, but she had an exciting life all over the world. I just loved her and hearing her stories. And she made me her Executor—except the term now is 'Personal Representative' or 'PR.' She had a really nice life, all in all, and also her death was pretty smooth and painless. . . . But the After Death is a 'rhymes with Witch.'"

"Oooh. How so?"

"So, Colleen did a Will on her own. It is just right, in that it has the right signing language and the right number of witnesses, and it waives bond for me as PR—that's common, I now understand. The Will has a bunch of bequests that do not conflict with each other—and she has enough money to satisfy all of them!—it sets up a Trust for a beneficiary whose money needs to be managed for her. And yet, and yet . . . the thing is going to be a brute to administer."

"Oh, really? Why is that?"

"The first thing is all the stuff she acquired over the years. I guess that's common with world travelers. Artwork, furniture, jewelry, fabric. And she had a bunch of friends. So, she makes tons of specific gifts. For example, she gives one gold bracelet to each of three particular friends."

"And the problem?"

"The problem is that we can find only two gold bracelets. How do we decide what to do about this? If she had only stated an order in which they could choose!

"Then she gives her guitar—I have a copy of the Will right here, so let me look at the exact language," she said, pulling it out of her purse. "Here: 'I give my Martin guitar to my buddy Jack Bolden.' But she didn't have a Martin guitar—she had a guitar, but it's a Fender. So, does Jack get the Fender, or was there something specific about the Martin that made her want him to have it?"

"Does he even want a guitar from her? Maybe the problem could be solved pretty easily," suggested Camille.

"I don't know yet, but that's sort of not the point. Then Colleen leaves all of her Thai artwork to one friend and all of her Nepalese artwork to another one. I know zippo about this, so I guess I need to get an art expert in to tell me which artwork is Thai and which is Nepalese."

"Wow. It would have been so helpful for her to have taken a picture of what was what and leave it with her Will. Or, better, to talk to you about this while she was still around to answer any questions."

"No kidding. You want another beer? Maybe some nachos?" offered Adrienne. "Anyway, there's the basic issue of 'If she no longer had it when she died, the person who was to get it gets nothing.' There's also the issue of the expense of shipping some of this stuff, if the person lives too far away to pick it up. I don't think the cost of sending a table to someone ever entered her mind, and her Will says nothing about who pays for shipping."

"OK," said Camille, "you're starting to hyperventilate! Take a sip of beer."

"Darn right, I am. And then we get into the rest of the Will, where she talks about money. Equally messy." Adrienne took a breath and a couple of swallows of beer. She consulted the copy of the Will.

"In her Will, Colleen makes a bequest of $30,000. Here's what the Will says: 'I give the sum of $30,000 to my cousin, Marie O'Brien.' So? you say. I say, well, Marie O'Brien just died, five weeks after Colleen. And there is nothing to limit the gift to Marie in the event of *her* death. So, this $30,000 will go to Marie's estate and to whatever beneficiaries Marie has named for her own assets.

"Rebecca Dalton—that's the lawyer I'm working with—says that a professionally prepared Will would prevent a bequest from going through two probate administrations by requiring a beneficiary to survive by some stated period of time—maybe 90 days or even longer. If you don't put some other survival period in your Will, the law in this state requires survival by only 30 days, and that's kind of short. In some places, it's 120 hours!!! So, Marie's Will gets to control this $30,000, instead of Colleen's. Nothing I can do about that one.

"Here's another thing—Colleen had lent money to some of her nieces and nephews. She directs me to distribute funds up to the amount of $20,000 to each niece or nephew, reduced by the amount of any outstanding loans she had made to them during her life. But the records I have been able to find are skimpy to nonexistent. I don't know if these loans have been repaid or not. Aaargh!!!!"

"I can't imagine a Court is going to want to decide something like this!" commented Camille.

"You're right—the Court won't want to! Then Colleen makes specific gifts of cash to people she knew in her travels. These are really tricky." Scanning her copy of the Will, Adrienne found the language she wanted: "Here's one: 'I give the sum of $25,000 to my friend, Madhu, also known as Matthew, who worked in my home in New Delhi when I was stationed there from 2000 to 2002.' And I absolutely can't find any address for this guy at all in her records. I don't even know if they were still in touch. As you see, I don't even know his family name. For all I know, maybe she didn't know it, either."

"Well, how are you supposed to be able to find him if she didn't even know where he was?"

"EXACTLY!!!!" exclaimed Adrienne.

"Do people think there's a big People Finder in the sky that Executors—excuse me, PRs—can consult to locate beneficiaries?" Camille wondered.

"It seems that way! I'm going to try to go through the State Department to see if possibly someone who was in India in 2000 or later might be willing to talk to me, if the State Department will even agree to help. Maybe diplomats share information about their household help, and someone else is in touch with Madhu. If this does not work, the Court might make me take out an ad in a New Delhi paper to find Madhu-Matthew.

"There's another bequest like that, for her housekeeper in Nepal, but that was more recent; we have a last name, and I found an address."

"This is turning into a full-time job," commented Camille.

"Right. This is why I have been sort of out of touch lately. And then there's one final thing. Whatever is left over after the other gifts are made, and the expenses of administering the estate are paid—including paying me!—will go to Colleen's sister Mary Ellen, and to her kids. Colleen left her sister one-third, then one-third to each child."

"And it turns out that there are three children, so she distributed four-thirds?" asked Camille.

"No, nothing that obvious—thank goodness! There are only two. But Mary Ellen's kids are totally different from each other. Tommy is a superstar—good in school, athletic, respectful, industrious—just an overall good guy. But Jessica is sort of the opposite—she's experimented with drugs, isn't much interested in school, and has run away a few times."

"So, Jessica's share has to be in Trust, or she'd just blow it all in a month?" observed Camille.

"Right! And, amazingly, Colleen's Will sets up that Trust. So that part is good. And the Will names Tommy to be Trustee."

"Oh, boy," said Camille. "So Tommy is supposed to manage Jessica's money, tell her when she can have some of it, and say 'No' to his sister! Whatever sibling issues they have already are going to explode completely."

"Yup. You got it immediately. I don't understand how Colleen could not see that. I don't think anyone, no matter how mature Tommy might be, could handle being the manager of funds for a resentful sister.

"It turns out we have a way out of this one, though. If Tommy chooses not to serve as Trustee, I get to pick who will serve in his place, and I'm even allowed to name myself. I don't really want to do it, but there won't be enough money to interest a bank in it, so I will consider it if Tommy makes that decision."

"Holy moly! You really have your hands full, here. C'mon over for supper, Adrienne. We can heat up some chili I have left from Sunday and watch a bad Netflix movie."

"Sounds great! Thanks for letting me talk your ear off!"

PORCH MUSINGS ON INTESTATE LAW

"Yup, intestate law—it's a funny thing," mused Ben Morgan, chewing on his cigar and sipping his Coors. He was waxing philosophical with his buddy Roger Bailey on a fine Spring afternoon, comfortably seated on the front-porch rocking chair.

Roger was comfortable too, leaning back, feet propped on the table, feeling no pain.

The men had resisted stretching their walk by a third trip around the block and had decided two turns earned them a cold one. They never had trouble finding a topic of discussion.

"So, why are you saying intestate law's so funny, Ben?"

"Aw, I was just reflecting on some of the cases that came into my office over the years. I was remembering one young gal. She was around 23 or 24, but she had heard about intestate law!!! I don't know if she had any money beyond next month's rent, but she was determined that her daddy wasn't getting any of whatever she did have."

"Just so I'm clear, you're talking about what happens if someone dies without a Will, right?"

"Yes. Well, this gal had found out that if she died without a Will, not survived by a husband or descendant, the law of this state would split her assets between her sainted mother and the bastard—that's her term, Rog—dad. She was still smarting from her parents' divorce and had developed a mean hate of her father for some reason. I didn't ask.

"Anyway, I told her there's nothing requiring you to leave money to any family member, except a spouse, of course, and even that can be waived in a marital agreement. We wrote up a Will leaving her entire estate to her mom, and if her mom did not survive her, to a charity. She signed with all the formalities, and she could rest easy. I think we did it all in three days, from her phone call to the signing!" noted Ben.

"Wow, it's amazing that she even thought about doing that. I don't think I'd know what would happen if I died without a Will."

"Heck, Roger, I think everyone should find out what would happen if they died without a Will. Every state has its own law of intestate succession. Maybe you'd be pretty upset about it. Or maybe you wouldn't. And it's not the same in every state. You might be surprised to know that a spouse doesn't necessarily get everything if you die without a Will. Sometimes it's a percentage, and that percentage might depend on whether the decedent, or the spouse, or the two of them together had any children."

Ben was feeling voluble. "Anyway, sometimes it's OK to not write a Will. Sometimes the state law provisions about what happens to a person's assets if that person dies without a Will are just what the prospective decedent wants, anyway. You know, ahem, a 'prospective decedent' is any client who's still alive."

"I got it, Ben."

Ben continued: "I remember getting a real excited call from a gal who was leaving for an extended trip to India in six days and realized that she did not have a Will. How you can fail to notice this until a week before you're going to a foreign land for a month is beyond me.

"Anyway, I asked the lady a couple of questions: Where do you live, who are your intended beneficiaries, how old are they, are there children of these beneficiaries?

"All of the answers were reassuring. She lived in Maryland, she was divorced, and she wanted her two adult daughters to share equally. Neither of them had children or had any illnesses or money-management issues. I told her, 'Have a good trip. The Will the legislature of Maryland wrote for you is just what you want. Your daughters will qualify as Personal Representatives, and they will share your estate, 50–50.' Then I told her, 'But be sure to do a real Will when you get back, to account for other contingencies.' She sounded so relieved! I probably could have sent her a bill then and there. Never did hear from her again, now that I think about it!"

Roger absorbed that. "Hmm. Well, my situation is like that one, so I'm feeling better already."

"Hah! Sorry, Roger—not so fast. Those little grandchildren of yours? They make a huuuuge difference. We should talk about it when we want to be serious. Later, maybe. For now, I'm just enjoying this smoke."

CINDY WRAPS HER BRAIN AROUND PROBATE

"So, if I have this right, it's just like everything I own is dropped into a big pot, and then it's divided up among various recipients, based on my Will, if I have one when I die, or based on the law of intestate succession, if I don't?" asked Cindy.

Cindy Fletcher is having Rebecca Dalton do her estate plan—all of this is new to Cindy.

"Yes, that's about it, with, of course, some exceptions. Your Will controls the items you own in your own name, but only those things. So, your bank account, your brokerage account, your condo would all be subject to your Will if they are in your individual name.

"But some things you might own don't go into the pot. For example, if you have an IRA, that does not go into the Probate pot. Granted, it's in your name, but, in truth, it's held by the IRA custodian or Trustee subject to a bunch of rules. So, for an IRA, you would name a beneficiary for the IRA, and the IRA goes to that person. If the IRA beneficiary designation said, 'Give my IRA to X' and the Will said, 'Give my IRA to Y,' it would go to X.

"Another thing that does not go into the pot is anything you own with someone else 'with right of survivorship,' if that other owner survives you," noted Rebecca. "So, you begin to see why the Will does not take care of disposing of all of your assets."

"OK. I see what you're saying. Tell me about what happens to the stuff that is in the pot," said Cindy.

"Sure. What happens to the 'pot' is called the Probate process. This is a Court proceeding that gives someone—the Executor, but we now call that person the Personal Representative, or PR—authority over those assets that were just in your name. Your bank can no longer deal with you if you're dead, so the Court appoints the person you name in your Will to take over, gives that person proof of appointment, and then the bank knows who has legal authority to close the account, manage any loan, and so on."

"The petitioner, who is the PR named in the Will, or, usually, a relative, if there is no Will, would normally have a lawyer help with filing a Probate petition. The petition tells the Court about your assets and liabilities, your heirs at law, the beneficiaries named in any Will, and other facts. If there is a Will, the petitioner files it at Court with the petition. The petitioner swears, either at Court or on paper, depending on the requirements of your state, to do the job as required by law."

"OK. I'm with you so far," said Cindy.

"Good. Next, there are costs in winding up an estate, so state law provides for these to be paid. Some Court costs are allowed right off the top—starting with a fee for filing the Court papers and the Will, if there is one, to start the Probate. The fee is based on the assets going through Probate, so it can be small or large, depending on your Probate assets.

"After the Court signs off on appointing the petitioner as PR, the PR will publish legal notices and send them to beneficiaries named in the Will, fiduciaries named in the Will, heirs at law, and creditors.

"After that, the PR starts doing what has to be done: taking control of your assets, making sure they are safe . . ."

Cindy interrupted: "What does that mean—'taking control'?"

"OK. Well, that means that the PR literally goes to, say, your bank, with the Court-issued proof—these are actual pieces of paper with the Court seal saying that your PR is acting for you, now that you have died. The PR also gives a death certificate to the bank so the bank can be doubly protected in dealing with your PR. Then, the bank closes the account in your name and gives a check for the proceeds to the PR.

"The PR gets a tax identification number for the estate from the I.R.S., sort of the estate's social security number, and uses that number to set up a bank account, brokerage account, and whatever other types of accounts might be needed. These assets are all titled in the name of your PR as PR of the Estate of Cindy Fletcher, and the PR reports all the income on tax returns he or she files for the estate. You don't want interest and dividends still coming in on the social security number of a person who has died!"

"What a thought!" said Cindy.

"So, then your PR just winds up everything. The PR pays your legitimate bills, including your final income taxes. The PR pays your funeral bill—funeral businesses all over the country have successfully lobbied state legislatures for laws making funeral payments, in full or in part, a preferred expense, so this is often one of the first bills paid. And the PR deals with any claims against the estate. Some might be invalid, so the PR has to figure this out.

"The PR needs to preserve your assets during the time the estate is administered. The PR will put the assets into fairly conservative investments. Some experienced PRs just liquidate everything and put the proceeds into some safe investment, even if it has a low yield. In an ordinary estate administration, it won't be invested very long before the estate is distributed to the beneficiaries. The PR has to beware of losing value but is not liable for failing to grow the assets as much as possible."

"What is the Court doing all this time?" asked Cindy. "Does it get regular reports on what is going on?"

"Well, yes. In some states," said Rebecca, "the Court requires regular reports, perhaps annually or more often. Other states require no reporting. The Court is available in case someone needs a ruling. For example, a beneficiary or an heir who thinks the PR is not doing the job properly might want to get a judge to look at the situation."

"Or, I suppose, the PR might need the Court to order some-one to turn over one of my assets to the PR?" asked Cindy.

"Yes, that could happen. Or, if the PR thought there was an ambiguity in the Will, he or she could ask the Court for guidance. Lots of stuff," said Rebecca.

"Now, one payment from the estate will be payment to the PR. This payment is governed by state law. In some states the PR gets paid a 'reasonable' amount—the PR has to keep track of what he did and the amount of time it took, and then get Court approval of an hourly rate. In some states, Court approval is not required, if the beneficiaries are notified and do not object and the fees are in a range that state law deems 'reasonable.' In other states, there is just a flat percentage. In some places, the lawyer also gets a flat fee! This is all a matter of state law, as is just about everything relating to Probate, so it's hard to make generalizations."

"This is really helping me understand the process. Thanks, Rebecca. If I end up in a state with high statutory fees, is there anything I can do to avoid them? Before I die, I mean."

Rebecca chuckled. "Yes, there is. Some people get assets out of Probate by setting up a Revocable Trust, which we can talk about later. In that case, you have the initial expense of setting up the Trust, which could be several times the amount of Court costs the estate will save—again, all depending on state law. But some of the expenses, like the funeral bill and the payment to the person winding up the decedent's affairs— these things still have to be paid, whether the assets are held in a Revocable Trust or go through Probate."

"Hmm," said Cindy. "OK, let me get clear on Probate before we start talking about how to avoid it! First of all, how long does all this take?"

"That's a common question!" noted Rebecca. "In most cases, you're looking at nine months to a year. But it can be years if the estate has fighting beneficiaries or PRs, or if there are complicated assets. I once got called in to work on an estate that was still open after ten years. There were tax issues, and there were significant non-U.S. assets, but the main problem was that there were thousands of artworks to dispose of."

"So, for me it would be more like a year, and you're saying that it might be even less. Tell me more about how the PR handles my bills."

"Sure. Some of your bills will be obviously legitimate. Those get paid. But someone, perhaps someone the PR didn't even know about, might file a claim against your estate. Creditors have a limited time in which to present a claim to the PR. This could be a couple of months, or even six months, depending on the law of your state. This is one of those things that varies widely with state law. And a secured creditor might have no time limit, because payment of the debt is mostly or completely covered through the mortgage, deed of trust, or whatever, and not through the individual assets of the decedent. Naturally, the tax authorities are likely to be creditors, and, of course, they often have a priority over other creditors."

"Whew. OK, that makes sense. When do my beneficiaries get into the picture?"

"Well, all through the Probate administration, the PR will likely be communicating with the beneficiaries, so they'll know what's going on. The rest of the pot, after Court costs, payment of taxes and bills, and payment to the PR, gets divided up for them. Again, there may be some priorities. For example, if you left a particular item to someone or made a bequest of a dollar amount, those distributions would take precedence over what we call the 'residue,' or the rest of your estate.

"I'd stress that this process takes place even if you die without a Will. After all those other payments are made, the PR liquidates your estate and writes checks to your heirs at law in the percentages set out in state law."

"Who are my heirs at law? And could I have another glass of water?" asked Cindy.

"Sure!" Rebecca asked her secretary to bring more water. Then she continued: "Now, you don't know who your 'heirs' are until you die. So, I guess, in a sense, you never do know. It depends on who among your relatives is living when you die. If you died today, single, with no children, your heirs would be your parents. If one of them died before you did, the surviving parent would be the sole heir. Basically, your 'heirs' are family members."

"OK, I understand. So, these are the folks who will get what I own when I die, if I don't have a Will—they could even be relatives I haven't seen for decades!" exclaimed Cindy.

Rebecca confirmed, "Oh, yes. They could be. That's one reason to review your estate plan regularly, to be sure your arrangements are set up to do what you want for the right people, in the right proportions."

"Food for thought!" said Cindy. "Thanks for the Probate tutorial. Let's get started on my Will!"

BEN AND ROGER DISCUSS WILLS

"I like hearing your war stories from your office days," exclaimed Roger. "How about a few more while we finish our walk?"

"Sure! You would be amazed at the kinds of serious problems smart people can create, all too innocently. I don't know if you know this, Roger, but hardly any lawyers will allow clients to sign a Will or a Codicil unsupervised."

"What!!! What could go wrong?" asked Roger.

"Well, the usual thing is that the client ignores some technical requirement. But sometimes there are other issues. Before I had this ironclad rule about supervising every client's Will signing, I once sent a Codicil to a super-sharp high school teacher to sign in her own home. She insisted that she would follow the instructions I included with the Codicil. I had all the instructions written out. You know: 'Have the witnesses in the room with you; tell them that this is a Codicil amending your Will'—they don't need to know what it says, mind you.

"And the instructions went on to say, 'Initial every page at the bottom, and then sign and date the Codicil where indicated on page 4; then have a witness date the witnessing language, and have the witnesses sign as witnesses and print their names and addresses below their signatures. Make sure that no witness is related to you and that no witness is named in the Will as either a beneficiary or fiduciary."

"Yeah?" asked Roger. "So, she didn't follow the instructions?"

"No, she followed every single instruction. But she signed in pencil. *Pencil*!! It had not occurred to me to say it should be signed in ink. When she sent me the Codicil for our file, I just could not believe it. She had a document that any malfeasor could invalidate by just applying an eraser!

"Most of the time, when people are sent Wills to sign, they will forget to initial a page, or they don't have the witnesses in the room with them. It's a rare experienced T&E lawyer who will let a testator supervise his own Will signing."

"Why do they have to initial every page?" asked Roger.

"Well, it's not a legal requirement, but it helps to confirm that each page in the Will filed with the Court was actually there when the testator signed it. If every page except one has an initial, the Court would want to know why this single page had no initial."

"What do you do if the testator is blind?" asked Roger.

"Ah, yes—this is tricky. We have our sighted clients read the document and ask us questions about anything they don't understand. But with a blind person, you want to take all the steps you can to ensure that the written material is conveyed to them by someone they trust fully. There are some blind folks who dispense with reading of some passages, like the fiduciary powers that are usually spelled out in a Will or Trust document. But any lawyer will insist that they hear the language distributing the assets and the terms of any Trusts in the Wills. So, these parts will be read to them—maybe by the lawyer or maybe by a family member. Of course, a lot of Wills are much longer than they need to be, and the reading can take a long time. Still, it really must be done, for the comfort of the client and the lawyer.

"Speaking of length, do you know why some documents have those antiquated phrases like 'I give, devise and bequeath'?" asked Ben.

"Not really. I just assumed this was all necessary," said Roger.

"Well, technically and historically, 'devise' and 'bequeath' were separate things, but 'give' can cover both. What I learned in law school is that these phrases we hear over and over were at some time in the past subject to lawsuits, probably because they were deemed ambiguous! In the course of the lawsuits, these phrases were ruled to have a particular meaning, now blessed by a Court. So, to stay on the safe side, lawyers keep using these phrases that had been subject to litigation, not because they are going to be clear to clients, but because, even if they are awkward, they have been determined to have a certain meaning that the lawyer wants to convey.

"Way too many lawyers rely on legalese. Clients hate it, it makes the documents twice as long as necessary, and it just kind of burns me up. When I was practicing, I considered it a badge of honor to be congratulated on the readability of a document I wrote."

"You know, Ben, you're onto something there," commented Roger. "I really think part of the reason Louise and I haven't been addressing our estate planning is that we dread having to read a bunch of stuff we're not going to understand."

TESTAMENTARY TRUSTS

How do you set up a Trust to take effect after you die? Why would you want a testamentary Trust? In what circumstances should your Will definitely have a testamentary Trust?

BEN AND ROGER DISCUSS TRUSTS FOR YOUNG FOLK

"The other day, you were talking about management of assets for grandchildren, Ben. You told me I needed to think about my grandchildren in drafting my Will. I don't really see why—their parents will take care of them."

Roger and Ben were back at it, enjoying the pleasant weather while circling the block for the first time.

"Yeah, well, when you commented that you might not need a Will, I thought I should straighten you out," said Ben. "Anyone whose estate might go to young beneficiaries needs to plan for management of their inheritance."

"Well," said Roger, "my wife Louise is still alive, and the kids are all grown, so my estate is not going to go to minors."

"You can't be sure about that, Roger. People die 'out of order' all the time. I can't tell you how often I had to work with parents burying their children—one of the hardest things I encountered in my law practice.

"If Louise died and then your daughter Adele fell off a cliff the day before you died, Adele's minor children, not her husband, would get Adele's share of your estate. If, for any reason, you did not, or could not, change your Will, your documents would need special arrangements for Adele's kids—what are they, two and four? Just out of curiosity, you do have a Will, right?"

"Oh, sure, but Louise and I did our Wills before we had any children," Roger said.

"You mean your Wills are 35 years old!?!? C'mon, Roger! You need to update those."

"I know. I think I named my father as Executor, and he died 20 years ago. But what's this stuff about grandchildren?"

"Well, you dodged a bullet in that Adele and John both reached the age of majority before you died, but you need to have a contingent plan for the grandchildren."

"A 'contingent plan'?" Roger interjected.

"I'm referring to a plan for managing assets that you want a grandchild to inherit if your child dies before you. If the grandkids are really young, your Will—and Louise's, too—should set up management arrangements for handling whatever you leave to the grandchildren.

"The usual arrangement is to have your Will set up one or more Trusts. You have lots of choices. For example, you could have one Trust for all grandchildren or for all grandchildren in one family. Or you could have a separate Trust for each grandchild. Or you could start with a group Trust and have it divide into separate Trusts when the youngest child reaches an age determined by you."

"Ben, I'm embarrassed to say this, but I don't really know how Trusts work," said Roger. "And I sure don't know how to 'set up' a Trust in my Will!"

"You're not alone there!" Ben exclaimed. "OK, let me explain. Think of a Trust as a little business under the control of the Trustee you name. The purpose of this little business is to take care of, say, your grandchildren, in accordance with your instructions. This purpose, the share of your estate dedicated to this purpose, the naming of the Trustee, and your instructions would be written into your Will. The instructions would be your ideas about what the Trust should be used for, put into legal language in the Will you would sign."

"All right. I've got it. *My* ideas, in *my* Will. I don't really have a lot of ideas here. I suppose I could talk to Adele to see what arrangements she and Adam have made in their estate plans," commented Roger.

"That's a great idea, coordinating the plans. It's not something I got to do much in my practice, because families are so spread out geographically, and they don't often think about this, but, in families who talk to each other, it's great to coordinate the parents' and grandparents' plans for the grandchildren.

"Anyway, one thing you would think about is how old you want the grandkids to be when they get full control of what you leave them," said Ben.

"Like age 50?" interjected Roger.

"Maybe! I once did a Trust that specified age 60 as the age for distribution! Anyway, at whatever age, the Trustee hands over any remaining Trust assets and closes out the Trust. Sometimes people have trusts that don't terminate but continue for the children of the grandchildren, and so on. I doubt that you would want anything that complicated."

"OK, Ben. But if I *don't* redo my Will, what is the downside? I'm not sure I really want to incur the expense," confessed Roger.

"The downside is that if one of your children dies before you—or even within a short time after you—you lose control over how a minor grandchild's money will be managed.

"Let's say Louise and Adele die before you die. I assume your Will would have Adele's share going to her children. But they're just little kids. So, someone has to go to Court to set up a Court-supervised guardianship for their money. And let me tell you, by the way, that's a *lot* more expensive than revising your Will now.

"The person who goes to Court could be Adam—but it might be some other family member, too—and let's say that you have always thought of Adam as clueless about money, or maybe a spendthrift. So, he's not necessarily the person you would pick to manage money for the kids. Maybe you would prefer to put your son John in charge of money for Adele's children.

"You can make sure that happens by setting up contingent Trusts for Adele's kids in your Will. They're 'contingent' because they come into existence only in the contingency that Adele—and Louise—die before you do, AND only for a child of Adele's who is under the age for distribution called for in the Trust," said Ben.

"Heck, I'm OK with Adam managing the money for his kids. What's so bad about this Court thing that I should do my Will over?" asked Roger.

"Hah! If you don't change anything—and excuse me, Roger, but I will call that the 'imbecile route'—if what I have just described happens, a Court-appointed guardian manages the money and then hands over what's left to each grandchild as the child reaches age 18. That's One Eight, Roger. And there might be a lot less left after all of the Court expenses involved in taking that route than there would be if you changed your Will now to set up contingent Trusts," cautioned Ben. "And did I mention that the guardian is appointed BY THE COURT!? Excuse me for yelling."

Roger got it: "You mean the inheritance could be reduced because of the cost of fidelity bonding, the Court costs, the costs of petitioning the Court for permission to spend the money, the cost of getting an approved investment plan for the grandchildren, and the cost of making annual accountings to the Court? I remember all that—you told me before. I'm just jerking your chain. I just never thought it would apply to me! I figured that, if one of my kids died before me, I'd change my Will then."

"You might not have that chance, Roger. You could be dead at the same time, or you could be mentally out of it. You and Louise need to update those old Wills—there could be other matters to attend to, too."

BART LEARNS ABOUT TESTAMENTARY TRUSTS

Rebecca took a call from her law school buddy, Bart Logan. "Bart! How's the divorce biz?"

"Highly charged, as always," said Bart. "Ha, just a little lawyer humor there. Seriously, we're doing a lot more collaborative divorces, which are much easier on the parties, and there's usually a better result for all concerned."

"That's great, Bart. I've heard of those, and I'm a fan. So, what's up?"

"Well, my father-in-law, Marge's dad, died last week. Marge just got a copy of his Will, and it calls for Trusts to be set up for our kids. So, I'm calling to see if you can draft those Trusts for us."

"Bart—I'm sorry for your loss. But as to drafting Trusts, there is no need for that. The terms of the Trusts are almost certainly in the Will. That's how they come to be called 'testamentary' Trusts—they're in the Last Will and Testament. How about sending me a copy of the Will—email is fine—and then call me in an hour, and we'll go over it together on the phone. By the way, you know the Will is a public document now that your father-in-law has died, or it will be as soon as the lawyer files it at Court, so you don't need to be concerned about confidentiality."

An hour later, Bart called back, and after confirming that he had a copy of the Robert Saul Goldman Will in front of him, Rebecca started to show him how to read it.

"OK, Bart—see, on page 12, Article Eight—there are provisions for fiduciary appointments. Your brother-in-law, Morton Goldman, is named to be his father's PR. And he is also named to be Trustee of any Trusts for Marge's kids. Marge is named to be Trustee of Trusts for Morton's kids.

"Then, Bart, turn to page 5, where, in Article Three, the language is set out establishing the Trusts. It says your father-in-law wants $100,000 of his estate to go to each grandchild if the grandchild is older than age 25, and into a Trust for the grandchild if he or she is younger than age 25. How old are your kids?"

"Marge and I have a 12-year-old and a 15-year-old."

"And Morton—what do we call him? Does he have kids?" asked Rebecca.

"Yes. Mort also has two children, but they are both over 25," responded Bart.

"OK, so no Trusts will be established for his children, and Marge will not be a Trustee. There will be only two Trusts established—one for each of your kids. What are their names, anyway?"

"Bart, Jr. is the 15-year-old, and his sister, Marilee, is 12 going on 30."

"Ah, yes—the sophistication of the preteen girl," commented Rebecca. "Anyway, here is how this happens: Mort, in his capacity as PR of his father's estate, is responsible for carrying out the terms of his dad's Will. That means he creates a Trust for each of your kids, probably naming it with the child's name, since no other name for each Trust is spelled out in the Will."

"What do you mean he 'creates' the Trusts?" asked Bart.

"Right. Since the terms of the Trusts are already in the Will, I should probably say that Mort is 'activating' the Trusts," said Rebecca.

"As PR of Mr. Goldman's estate, Mort will soon, or maybe already has, set up a bank account in his name as PR of the Probate estate, using the tax ID number for the estate. Then he will apply to the IRS for tax ID numbers—those are like social security numbers—for the Bart Logan, Jr. Trust and the Marilee Logan Trust. That's for reporting income in the Trusts. He uses those numbers to set up a bank account for each Trust in his name as Trustee.

"His next step is to transfer $100,000 out of the Probate estate into each Trust account. And after that, he goes about managing the assets in each Trust. So, he has to decide how to invest the Trust funds in a way that is prudent and consistent with having liquidity available when needed for the Trust purposes. He has to keep you—and, when they are older, your children—advised of the assets, liabilities, expenditures, and income of each Trust."

"OK, Rebecca. I'm following you so far. And what are the Trust purposes?"

"The directions for what the Trustee is to do are also in Article Three of the Will. If you read there, in line two, it says the Trustee can use the money for, and I'm quoting, 'medical expenses, music lessons, and two weeks of summer camp each year.' That's quirky, but there's nothing illegal about it. I suppose he figured you had education expenses covered?" Rebecca asked.

"Yes, he knew that Marge and I had a fully funded 529 plan for Bart Jr.'s college and are almost there on Marilee's 529 plan." Bart then asked, "So, if Bart, Jr. decides to go to computer camp in Sweden, he can just withdraw the money for the travel, the cost of the camp, and any other expenses he might incur?"

"Oh, no—not at all. The Trust terms do not allow the beneficiary to 'withdraw' anything. The control is all in your brother-in-law's hands. If Bart, Jr. wants to go to that camp, he can pitch his case to Mort, but if Mort somehow thinks this goes beyond his authority as Trustee—or if the cost would wipe out the Trust long before Bart, Jr. turned 25—he can refuse. It's not up to Bart."

"I see."

Rebecca said, "OK, now look at Article Fifteen. On pages 15 to 17, the Will sets out the powers of the Trustee. The stated powers are fairly broad, but not unlimited—for example, there is a prohibition on buying commodities with Trust funds, and margin loans are also prohibited. The powers of the Trustee written here are fairly standard and are a reference for Mort as he manages these Trusts."

"So," asked Bart, "Mort can just refer to this Will for everything he needs to know to act as Trustee?"

"No, unfortunately, not exactly everything. In addition to the written provisions, state law has requirements of Trustees like Mort. For example, Mort needs to inform you or Marge as a competent parent, about what he is doing on behalf of your children. This is referred to in the Will but not spelled out. It's in state law.

"As I mentioned earlier, this reporting involves regular accountings of each Trust's assets, liabilities, income, and the expenditures Mort is making. He'll probably do this by giving you copies of the brokerage and other account statements. He has to notify you if he moves, and so on. And, of course, inasmuch as each Trust is a taxpayer, Mort as Trustee has to file income tax returns for the income earned in each Trust, at both the state and federal level, unless the income is so little it's below the filing threshold."

"Hmm," said Bart, "I see that this is quite a job. I note that he can be paid for his work—page 14 says that, as long as his pay is 'reasonable.' But he's already told us he isn't going to take any compensation, just reimbursement for expenses."

"That's nice," said Rebecca. "So, now let's look at the Will language discussing the ending of each Trust. At the end of Article Three, it says that, when each child reaches age 25, Mort turns over to the child whatever remains in the Trust in his or her name. We don't know how much that might be—it's conceivable that it could be more than the Trust started with, if Mort invests well, the stock market booms, and the child didn't need to use much of the Trust. OR, it could be a lot less. You see here on page 16, in the powers provisions, that, if Mort deems the Trust to be too small to continue, like less than $10,000, he can terminate it and distribute the remaining funds to the child as long as the child has reached age 21."

"Wow—how do you grasp all this stuff?" marveled Bart.

"Years of experience. And after you have read it a few times, it will get clearer for you, too. And it will get clearer for Mort as he continues to act in accordance with his duties under this document."

"Well, better Mort than me, I'd say. By the way, Marge is coming into some nice money as a result of her father's death—Mort says distribution won't be for at least six months, but we want to plan. So, we'll be setting up an appointment with you to review our estate plan. We haven't looked at it since Marilee was a year old!"

"Bart!!! Typical lawyer, you. Happy to help."

BEN AND ROGER DISCUSS TRUSTS, PART TWO

"OK, buddy. I've been thinking about these Trusts you say I need to add to my estate plan because I have grandchildren. Now I want to know more about my options," said Roger. Ben and Roger were in Roger's house after a game of gin rummy, sipping iced tea.

"You got my attention when you said we were lucky, living to see our kids become adults. And the same issue applies to John and Adele—they might not still be around and 'with it' when their kids are launched, either. It's just that you have certain expectations, you know?"

"I know, Roger, and it makes a convenient excuse for not dealing with the idea of what happens when the world goes on after you're out of it. Still, after practicing T&E law for decades, I often saw people feel pretty good about themselves when they had finished their estate planning. Responsible, competent, on top of things—you know."

Ben went on: "Anyway, Rog, here's the deal with testamentary Trusts. They are always at least in part about *management* of money or other assets. There are dozens of reasons you might want management, but there are two main ones. The first is, the beneficiary can't be trusted with managing money for himself. Here, the typical example is a young beneficiary."

"Like grandchildren," noted Roger. "But I suppose that would cover a lot of other folks, too."

"You bet," said Ben. "You could be concerned that a beneficiary might have some kind of problem—like drug dependence, being profligate with money, a bad marriage that might lead to a bad divorce, susceptibility to scams, whatever—you can set up a Trust for dealing with those, too. You aren't exactly controlling the money from the grave, but it's the next best thing!"

Roger commented: "Man, this could be really valuable. Louise was telling me about some friend of hers whose sister is addicted to opioids. You sure would not want to give someone like that free rein over a chunk of money."

"Yes, this is a serious problem, all right. But, on the hopeful side, you can, with thought, put provisions into your Will that will allow the control to end when it seems prudent to end it. For minors, you might allow them to have the money at age 25, or maybe part at age 25, more at age 30, and the rest at age 35—that's called a 'serial distribution.' You can even allow the Trustee some flexibility with these terms, but, of course, how convoluted you want to make such a Trust is partly a function of how big the Trust is."

"Huh," said Roger. "That's kind of interesting. I guess I can see why you'd want to talk to a lawyer who does this all the time—I wouldn't have thought about all these options."

"Sure," said Ben, continuing. "You just sit with a lawyer and have a conversation about your concerns. For example, if you're setting up a Trust for someone suffering from an addiction, you might even let the Trustee hand out money if the beneficiary passes certain drug tests you write into the document to show that they have shaken off the addiction. There's a lot of latitude."

"Want some more iced tea, Roger? Cookies to go with that?"

"Nope. I'm good, thanks."

"OK." Ben asked, "What is the second reason for management you were talking about as to testamentary Trusts?"

"Oh, yes. Well, sometimes you want a person to have the benefit of Trust funds for their lifetime but you want to control the disposition of whatever is left when they die. So even if the person *could* handle finances, you don't want them to. I'm not saying this applies in your case. I'm just being thorough, since we're on the topic.

"A typical example is a second marriage situation, especially where there are children with a prior spouse. So, a guy could write a Will that would establish a testamentary Trust for the new spouse, if she survived. I say "she." In estate planning, we tend to assume the wife survives, for some reason. I stopped objecting a long time ago. Anyway, a Trustee manages money for the surviving spouse to keep her comfortable, and then, when she dies, the Trustee distributes the remaining Trust assets to the man's descendants.

"You can see that if he gave her all the money outright, it could end up with *her* children, not his. Even if they're on great terms, anything could happen—the stepchildren might lose contact with her, or she could remarry, for example."

"But why wouldn't I want Louise to have all my money?"

"Maybe, in your case, you would be happy to give Louise all your money, but sometimes, even in a first-and-only marriage, people want to control their assets beyond the life of the surviving spouse. For one thing, Louise could remarry. I suppose you didn't think about that! And in the reverse situation, Louise could have money of her own that she would not want your next wife to get.

"Your case aside, think of a childless couple. They might plan to leave everything to charitable causes, but spouse A likes one charity, and spouse B likes a different one. Or if it's not charity, they have different family members to whom they want to leave their assets. If they leave everything to whichever spouse survives, the first decedent's choice of beneficiaries could end up with zippo."

"But what if the spouse predeceases—how do you like it that I know that word!?" asked Roger.

"Very impressive, Roger. You get a gold star. So, if the spouse predeceases, then the Trust for the spouse does not get activated, and you just skip over to the next provisions of the Will. A Will should always provide for reasonably possible contingencies—spouse predeceasing, even a child predeceasing.

"For example, I might leave my brother $10,000 'if he survives me' (Ben made airquotes), and if he does not survive me, the money goes to other beneficiaries. And along the same lines, a Will could say, in effect: 'I leave assets in a Trust for my wife if she survives me, and if not, I give my estate to my descendants. See provisions below for terms of Trust and for terms of gifts to my descendants.' The wording would not be exactly that, but you get the idea," said Ben. "And you always provide for management of assets for young grandchildren in the event your child who is their parent dies before you. It happens, as much as you don't want to think about it."

"I'm a little slow here, Ben, but I'm beginning to get it. You are making the point that I can do a lot to control what happens to my assets if one of our kids dies before I do, or maybe after I die but before Louise does. And the share of that child could go to minor kids who can't manage it!!! Wow! Thanks, Ben."

"Bravo, Roger. You're a quick study."

"OK, Ben. It's not a fun thing, but if you'll give me Rebecca's phone number, I'll call and set up an appointment."

"You're really going to do it this time?"

CHAPTER
THREE

JOINT OWNERSHIP AND SIMILAR ARRANGEMENTS

What are the risks and rewards of putting assets into joint names? Does the term "joint property" mean the same thing all over the U.S.? What happens with jointly held assets when one of the joint owners dies? Is Payable on Death the same as joint ownership?

MRS. BARTLETT SCREWS UP HER ESTATE PLAN

Amy glanced at the display on her phone and picked up: "Hi, Jen."

"Hi, Amy. Listen, I'm calling because Mom is in the hospital."

"What?! What happened?"

"Well, she had a bad fall in the kitchen. I had been trying to reach her all day to follow up something we were talking about last night, but she wasn't answering. After the soup kitchen called at three o'clock to see if I knew why she wasn't there for her weekly volunteer service, I went to the house. I found her on the floor—it looks like she slipped and hit her head on the granite countertop. So, I called 911 and got her into the hospital. She's not doing well. I think you should come. I'm calling Beth, too."

Two days later, the three of them were resting in Mom's house when the call came from the hospital. Mom had died peacefully. They were glad they had all had a chance to visit in the hospital and speak with Mom briefly, but it was just so sudden, it was hard to know what to do.

The next afternoon, after the three of them had had a chance to absorb the news, they realized they needed to arrange a funeral. Jen, who had lived in town with Mom, knew where in Mom's desk to find her funeral wishes, and they had even had a couple of conversations about what they would each want in a funeral. Mom was nothing if not organized—everyone knew that about Mrs. Bartlett. Jen, Amy, and Beth were glad their mother had been so responsible about her future after their father died.

The sisters were glad they got along so well. They made arrangements to stay in town for a week after the funeral to get started on sorting out their mother's estate. There, right in Mom's desk, was a file called "Will." Leave it to Mom. They pulled it out and read the copy of the Will, which noted that the original signed Will was with the lawyer.

Sure enough, Mom had gone to a lawyer after Dad's death, to make sure everything was up to date. The three daughters were named as co-Executors, and they were equal beneficiaries, after $25,000 to Mom's church and another $25,000 to her college. This was comforting, and it was just what they had expected from Mom. The lawyer's business card was with the Will. They set up a meeting for the day after the funeral.

The lawyer, Rebecca Dalton, welcomed the three daughters, said how sorry she was to learn about Mrs. Bartlett's death, and offered them tea or coffee. After they were all settled in the conference room, the daughters asked Rebecca what they had to do to proceed. Amy commented, "Well, she left a Will, so thank goodness we won't have to go through Probate!"

Rebecca corrected her, gently. "Hmm. Well, that's a common misconception, but a Will does not keep you out of Probate Court. It just tells the Court and the Executor how to distribute the assets that are subject to the Court's jurisdiction."

"Oh, golly—we have to go through Probate!!??" the daughters said, almost simultaneously, shaken.

"Well, yes, but that is nothing to worry about. Here, in the District of Columbia, the usual Probate involves preparing a basic petition to the Court for authority to carry out the terms of the Will, publishing and mailing legal notices, and within 90 days certifying to the Court that the notices have been given. The people who get notices are the named beneficiaries, the fiduciaries, the heirs at law—that's the three of you—and creditors. When you have done all that, you have no more reporting requirements to the Court. It's more complicated in other states, but simple here. That's it for 'Probate.'"

"Well, that doesn't sound too bad. How much does it cost, and what is the point of a Will if you still have to go through Probate?" asked Jen.

Rebecca explained: "Well, there is a filing fee, but it depends on the assets going through Probate, so I can't answer that right now. A few hundred dollars, probably, in your mother's case.

"As for 'Why have a Will if you have to go through Probate anyway?', it's to make provisions to suit your particular situation. For example, your mother wanted to give money to her church and school. When you have a Probate and no Will, the state or, here, DC, law directs where your money will go. In this case, that means the three of you would inherit equally but there would be no charitable bequests."

"Oh, OK. I guess the Probate process does not sound too bad, if there are basically only two Court contacts and no more reporting or supervision," the girls agreed.

"Well, here are Mom's financial records, as you requested, and the bill from the funeral company," Jen said, handing over four neat files from Mom's desk, along with the bill from Gentle Rest Funeral Home.

Rebecca gathered the daughters' addresses and other information for the Probate petition. "Thanks," she said. "I'll look over this financial information, prepare the Probate petition, and have you come in to sign it tomorrow. We'll file it at Court, and, in about ten days, the three of you can begin your official duties, after the judge reviews the petition and signs off."

Rebecca called the next day. Jen answered.

"Hi, Jen. I'm ready to meet with you and your sisters. Can you come in around three o'clock?"

Now that the sisters had had some time to adjust to the death of their mother, they were taking comfort in being together, telling old family stories over meals, and looking at Mom's jewelry and clothes to figure out what each of them might want. It had been a healing time.

But Amy and Beth, who lived three and five hours away, were ready to move the Probate process along and get back to their "real" lives. Jen, who was single, and whose "real" life had involved a lot of time with Mom, was grieving the loss of her parent and also the loss of certain routines in her life. She and Mom had always had dinner together on Monday nights, and this had become a sacred ritual after Dad died. They generally went out for these occasions, checking out new restaurants, sometimes adding a movie into the mix.

The sisters reconvened in Rebecca's office. When they had dispensed with the pleasantries, Rebecca handed out copies of the Probate petition she had prepared, and they all took a look at it.

"So," she started, "you see that this form spells out everything you need to get the Probate going. On the front page, we have your Mom's name, address, and age, where and when she died, and the fact that she had this Will, with its date. We have to submit the original Will with this Probate petition—a copy won't do. But we have made a copy for each of you.

"Then, in the rest of the form, we have a list of her heirs at law—that's the three of you—and beneficiaries—the three of you, the church, and the college, with everyone's addresses. Then we list her assets and her creditors, including the funeral home, and you all sign to agree to do the job of administering the estate."

"Um, Rebecca," started Beth, "the only assets listed here are the house and 'tangible personal property,' whatever that is. What about her financial assets?"

"Yes, we'll discuss that in a moment. The papers you brought in indicate that your mother's assets are worth about $1.6 million, of which some $900,000 or so is the value of the house, which has no mortgage. The rest is in various kinds of financial accounts with a brokerage firm and a couple of banks.

"Now, here's the thing. The financial assets don't have to go through Probate."

"Cool!" the girls agreed.

"Well, not so cool. On this, I have good news and bad news. The good news is that your mom had an IRA she inherited from your father. It is now worth about $180,000 and is managed by Multistate Mutual Fund Company. The three of you are beneficiaries."

"So, we don't have to file a Probate petition for that?"

"No, it's yours as of the date your mother died. You will file a death certificate—an official one, with the raised seal—with Multistate Mutual Fund Company. They will ask a bunch of questions, like confirming your addresses and social security numbers. They will also discuss your options for how you want the account distributed. You do have some flexibility for keeping the account in your name, earning tax-deferred income for a while. Of course, when you take the money out, you pay tax on it.

"At any rate, the beneficiary designation form your mother filed names you to be the principal beneficiaries at your Mom's death. All of you survived her, so each of you will receive one-third of the account. As I say, your mother owned the account, in the sense that she had control over who gets it, but it is not considered part of your mother's Probate estate. It does not go through Probate at all, and is not subject to the Court's jurisdiction."

"Hmm. I think I get that," noted Beth, "What about the other accounts?"

"OK. Jen, were you aware that your mother had put your name on her checking account?"

"Oh, sure. She wanted me to be able to write checks to pay her bills, in case she was ever incapacitated." Here, Jen started to sniff a little, and her eyes got red. "Anyway, we went into the bank to set this up, and we talked to a young lady at one of the desks. She told Mom the easiest way to take care of this was to put my name on the account, so that's what we did."

"I see," said Rebecca. "And your mother asked you to do this because you lived in town and it would be more convenient for you than for your sisters, I assume."

"Oh, yes. I told her I'd be happy to take care of her bills if the time ever came that she needed help. But, fortunately, she went out on a high note and handled her own bills the whole way. Oh, I miss her so much!"

Beth and Amy asked, at about the same time, "So, what does that mean? We don't understand the significance of what you're telling us."

Rebecca said, "And the lady at the bank probably didn't, either. It's like these bank people never heard of powers of attorney. Here's the bad news I mentioned earlier: By putting Jen's name on the account, your mother made Jen an owner of the account equal to herself."

"OK. So I could write checks on the account to pay Mom's bills. What's wrong with that? And I really never had to do that!" protested Jen.

"Right," said Rebecca. "And you had the power to write checks on the account to pay your own bills, too! Not that you would do that. However, you are now legally the owner of whatever remains in the account."

"Me, Amy, and Beth, you mean."

"No, just you," said Rebecca.

"But here's the really bad news. For the checking account, which is only $20,000, we don't need to get tied in knots. But Jen, your mother apparently thought it was such a benefit to her that you have that ability that she went to the brokerage firm and added your name to that $500,000 account, too. The reason the brokerage and checking accounts do not go through Probate is that you, Jen, personally and alone, are now the owner of those accounts as of your mother's death."

"WHAT!!!???" the three sisters cried in unison.

DIS-JOINTING

"Francine, can you come over this afternoon? I have to talk to someone!"

"Well, sure, Abby—two o'clock? Do you want me to bring anything?"

"Two is good. No, I don't need anything other than your good judgment and a shoulder to cry on."

"Oh, dear!" said Francine. "I'll be there."

Francine arrived on the dot, with a plate of chocolate chip cookies. Abby made some tea to go with them.

"So, what's up, Abby? You sounded a little distraught on the phone."

Abby started to sniff. "It's my joint accounts! I had no idea what a problem I was creating! You know, I wanted to keep my estate out of Probate, and Marianne said she did that by making all of her assets joint with her son.

"Anyway, I decided to put my son and grandson on the condo deed, so they could have it when I die. It was really easy to do. I just took my old deed to a lawyer who used the language from the old deed to make a new deed. I signed it. Bill and Harry didn't have to sign. In fact, they don't even know I did this. Filing it at the Recorder of Deeds was cheap, and it was all done. Between the lawyer and the filing fees, it was less than $400."

"That sounds like a nice thing to do for them, all right."

"Sure. But now I want to put my condo into a Revocable Trust."

"I have a Revocable Trust," said Francine. "I think that's a better way to go than joint property. But are you saying you have some kind of problem?"

"Yes! I found out the condo isn't mine!!!!"

"Abby, take a breath, and slow down. What do you mean, it isn't yours?"

Abby moaned. "Hah. I just thought I could transfer the condo into my name as Trustee of my Trust, but it turns out I gave away that authority. I thought the joint ownership would just take effect at my death, but nooooo. It took effect the moment I signed the deed and it was filed at the Recorder of Deeds office."

"Well, can't you just do a new deed?"

"That's the problem! I can't do it alone. In order to change ownership back to me so I *can* do a new deed, I have to get Bill and Harry to sign off. They are actual owners of the property, with me, and they have to decide it's OK for me to have my own apartment back in my own name—or my own Trust, in this case. I mean, *they own it, too*!!!!"

"Whew! Wow. That's the very definition of 'No good deed goes unpunished.' They *will* sign off to give it back to you, won't they?" asked Francine.

"I don't know!!! Bill and I had a little spat a couple of weeks ago, and I don't really even want to ask him. I'm just sorry I did this in the first place." Abby sniffled.

"Umm, not to create a further problem, but what about Harry?" asked Francine.

"What do you mean, 'What about Harry?'" asked Abby.

"Well, it occurs to me, isn't he only like ten years old?"

"Yeah—he's 11, but I'm sure he'd be willing to sign his interest over to me, whenever I get up the nerve to ask him."

"Well, I don't mean to stir the pot here," hesitated Francine, "but I don't think he can do that. Legally, I mean. I don't think he's deemed to be an adult. I'm not sure his signature will be effective, since he's still a minor until he's 18."

"OH, NO! I hadn't even thought about that," agonized Abby. "You mean I really have lost control of everything? I put both my son and grandson on as joint owners of my mutual funds and a checking account. Are they in control of those, now, too?"

"Joint ownership is tricky, all right. I'm pretty sure that there's an easy solution with the checking account. You might be able to just withdraw the money and set up a new account in your own name—or in your name as Trustee of your new Revocable Trust. But I have a feeling that on the real estate—and maybe the mutual funds—you're going to have to talk to a lawyer. Getting authority to act for a minor is kind of a big deal, when the asset is in the minor's own name."

"Man, I wish I had talked to you earlier, Francine. Now my 'simple solution'"—Abby did the air quotes—"has led to a very NON-simple disaster, and I'm just soooo annoyed with myself."

"Well," consoled Francine, "at least nobody died or went to prison!"

"Thanks. I guess I need to keep perspective," said Abby. "What a mess. I think I'll have another cookie."

WHAT ARE THE "ODS"?

Roger had just trounced Ben in a two-hour game of gin rummy and was getting them some tea and a plate of Louise's cookies, when a thought popped into his head.

"Ben, what is this stuff about 'POD'? My buddy, Max, told me he had a 'POD' account with his son, and I was too embarrassed to ask what that was. He made it sound like a big deal—it was going to keep him out of Probate, and it had been recommended to him."

"Ah, OK. Well, first, it's pronounced 'Pee Oh Dee,' not 'Pod.' And second, yes it does keep an account out of Probate, although the account funds might still be considered available to pay creditors. The POD stands for 'Payable on Death.' But if your friend Max made only that one account POD, he might still have other assets to go through Probate.

"Did he tell you who recommended this step to him? Putting an 'on death' designation on all your assets can be a huge mistake if it doesn't fit your estate plan. You'd be surprised at how many advisers recommend such changes without even looking at the estate plan. Sometimes the 'OD' designations will ruin the plan completely!"

"How is that? You mean I can't change just a part of my plan?" asked Roger.

"Sure, you can, Rog, but either you or your estate planning lawyer should make sure a 'Payable on Death' or 'Transfer on Death'—that's for brokerages—designation doesn't move assets away from where they're needed. For example, if your Will had a bequest to me—and go right ahead and put one in, if you like—but all of the assets were 'POD' or 'TOD' to other people, there wouldn't be anything to cover the bequest. A bigger problem is that these designations can remove all liquidity from an estate, so there's nothing to pay basic expenses, like a few mortgage payments before a house can be sold."

Roger looked concerned. "You know, we expect these folks who deal with money issues all the time to look out for our interests. Or at least to understand the things they are recommending! I mean, if there's no liquidity, who pays for this stuff?"

"Right!" said Ben. "Well, if there's no liquidity, you have to get a loan for the estate from somewhere or sell some illiquid asset—it creates problems, all right. But someone whose job is insurance, or a broker, or even some financial planners—they aren't always trained to look at this part of the picture. They have other expertise. Ideally, you have a team, and that implies teamwork—they work together and let the estate planning attorney coordinate the plan. You know, so that it really is a 'plan' and not just a conglomeration of financial arrangements.

"Anyway, here's how the POD works. Max went to his bank—maybe he has a big savings account or something—and told the bank to make his son an immediate beneficiary of the account effective at Max's death."

"So, it's like a beneficiary designation?" asked Roger.

"No, not exactly. A 'beneficiary designation' is *required* for retirement plans, for annuities, and for other insurance products, so the institution holding the funds knows where they should go when you die. A POD designation is voluntary, and if none is made, the bank account simply becomes part of your estate, subject to your Will. Still, the POD works the same way as a beneficiary designation, in that, at Max's death, his son takes Max's death certificate to the bank, and the bank hands over the money to the son."

"So, isn't the POD a sweet and simple way to get out of Probate?" asked Roger.

"It works fine for that single asset. And several states let you have an 'On Death' designation for a car, which is kind of handy. But you can just about never be sure you are providing for all assets. I mean, you're still in Probate if you have some other asset in your name, maybe a stock certificate, or somebody owes you money, or you have a house, or another bank or brokerage account, or a tax refund comes in after you die. You get the idea.

"I mentioned earlier the TOD. That's 'Transfer on Death'—it's like 'Payable on Death' for brokerage accounts. And—here's some breaking news, Roger—about half the states even allow you to deed a piece of real property to a child or someone else in such a way that it's yours while you are alive and then belongs to the child or whomever when you die. That's a Transfer on Death deed. Title companies aren't crazy about them, so we like to restate the transfer in the Will—but these things exist!"

"Heck, I can't see giving my kids control of my brokerage account while I'm alive!! No way!" exclaimed Roger. "And certainly not my house!"

"Well, hold on," said Ben. "The thing with all of these 'On Death' arrangements is that you can change them while you're alive. You're not giving up control. The kids or whatever other beneficiaries you have named have no control until you die. So, you're right—they can be a nifty tool for avoiding Probate. But when you set up one of these, you are cutting out other beneficiaries, so you need to be sure you're not skewing the balance of where your assets will end up. And, of course, you aren't providing for management of these assets, either."

"Oh, right. We have talked about managing assets," noted Roger.

"AND," continued Ben, "sometimes the institutions holding the funds don't really want to let go. I have heard of some reputable large money managers that just don't let go of the TOD funds right away. They keep coming up with new requirements, when all they should need is a death certificate and the correct contact information and tax ID for the beneficiary. In one case I know of, a big family of mutual funds still had not turned over the money in the funds seven months after the decedent died."

"That's outrageous! What if the beneficiary really needed the money?"

"I don't know," said Ben. "This 'gatekeeper' problem is often lamented among estate planning attorneys. You would probably be surprised at how often we have to threaten litigation just to get banks, brokers, money managers, and others to do after their client's death what they had promised to do while the client was alive. I suppose they're worried about making a mistake.

"Sometimes they *should* worry, because they don't seem to understand the situation. I have heard of banks asking for a copy of a Trust agreement, when they already had the copy of the Probated Will establishing the Trust in their possession."

"Yikes, Ben. Have another cookie."

"No, thanks. Marianne will smell them on my breath, and I'd better think about getting home. I demand a rematch on the rummy tomorrow!"

BENEFICIARY DESIGNATIONS

Can you make anyone the beneficiary of an IRA? Is it really necessary to read the beneficiary designation form from your well-established big-name family of funds before you sign it? What are the main differences between life insurance beneficiary designations and retirement plan/IRA beneficiary designations?

WHO'S THE BENEFICIARY?

Zoe is working with her Major Brokerage account manager, Henry, to complete the beneficiary designation for the rollover IRA she set up when she left her corporation. It has $800,000 of assets.

"OK, Henry. So I want my kids, Ken and Barbie, to be my primary beneficiaries, and if they die, their kids."

"They both have children?"

"Yup. Ken has two, and Barbie has one."

"OK, great. Well, we'll just take care of that right here. Mmm—filling in blank 1, Primary: Ken and Barbie; filling in blank 2, Secondary: Bob and Carol and Ted. OK, sign here, and I'll get this filed at HQ."

"Thanks, Henry."

A week later, Zoe was on the phone, in a panic: "Henry! I need to talk to you!"

"What's going on, Zoe?" asked Henry.

"Well, I gave a copy of my beneficiary designation form to my kids, and Barbie—she reads everything—she read it very carefully."

"Good! That's what we want, isn't it?"

"Well, yes, but what you wrote on the form does not do what you told me. You know that my intention was to have the IRA pass down half to each child, and if one child died before me, the children of the deceased child."

"Yeeess?"

"If you read your form, which, I'm happy to say, Barbie did, it says something totally different. If she died before me, my son Ken would get her share, not her son Ted."

"Really?"

"Yes. Only if both Ken and Barbie died before me would anything go to the grandchildren."

"Both Ken and Barbie??!!" asked Henry.

"Yes! And then the grandchildren's shares would be in thirds, which is not what I wanted. To be fair—or to do what

I wanted, Ken's half should go to his kids, Bob and Carol, even if Barbie is still alive when I die, and Barbie's half should go to Ted. You need to fix this!!!"

Later, in a meeting with Rebecca Dalton to review the entire estate plan, Zoe learned that this is exactly how some of the large mutual fund firms set up their form IRA beneficiary designations. This is not what many clients expect.

"'Read the Form.' That's my mantra," said Rebecca. "People say, 'It's only a form.' It looks official. It looks benign. It looks like you aren't allowed to modify the printed parts. It leaves hardly any room for all the information the company needs about each beneficiary—full name and address, social security number, birthdate, relationship. But you need more options. Fortunately, we have had luck getting some companies to accept attachments."

"OK, then—could you send this in for me?" asked Zoe.

Rebecca groaned. "I can, but I want to warn you that this is just the start of a negotiation—it could be long; it could be short. Beneficiary designations can be a lot more time-consuming to get right than clients expect. Sometimes there are multiple exchanges between the financial institution and the lawyer. But it's your money they are holding, and you're entitled to full cooperation. People think 'It's just a form,' but in your case, this 'form' is disposing of, maybe $800,000! That's real money."

"No kidding!" said Zoe. "Just out of curiosity, what do you do if you can't get the company to fix it the way I want it?"

"I sometimes recommend to clients that they threaten to move their IRA to another institution. If enough money is involved, that will get their attention. If not, you move it.

"The big problem with these form designations, though, is that sometimes you don't know you have a problem until it's too late to fix it. It's really important to read the form carefully—or have a daughter like Barbie, who will read it! But most people would not think of that—they'd just assume that the company knows what you would want."

"I don't think I'll make that mistake again!" said Zoe.

DESIGNATIONS OVER DINNER

Rebecca and Ben meet for dinner at Café Extraordinaire. They have not talked for a couple of months and are looking forward to seeing each other. Rebecca had a bee in her bonnet.

"Ben," she asked, "did you ever have trouble with beneficiary designation forms when you were in practice?"

"Oh, yes—all the time," he said. "It is amazing how persistent the problems are, and they often seem to boil down to one thing: the holiness of The Form."

"Oh, boy. That's exactly my point. People see that four-page sacred form from some major money management company, and they think a) the company kind of knows what the customer wants, anyway, b) they should be able to squeeze all of their wishes into the two lines provided, and c) they don't need to read the teeny print."

"Bingo!" said Ben. "I remember a lady who had put her entire corporate retirement plan into an IRA. It was close to a million. She had retired from BIG Corp. a couple of years before and assumed she'd be fine moving her retirement funds to an IRA with a major money manager. She wanted her kids to get the IRA, and if they weren't alive, their children. And that's what the form said, all right!"

"Let me guess," commented Rebecca. "The form said that nothing goes to the secondary beneficiaries unless *all* of the primary ones have died before Mom. I had that very situation today! Fortunately, the IRA money manager of the client I saw today was amenable to making a change. But the client was rattled, I would say!"

Ben offered Rebecca some more wine. "I'm sure you have seen the other common problem with these forms—lack of space on the printed form to spell out your wishes. In other words, sometimes people accept that they have to change their wishes just because the form doesn't give them enough room to put in what they really want!"

"Yes, I've seen that, too," Rebecca said. "For some reason, they just have faith that the teeny print says what they want it to say, and, if it doesn't, that they should decide to want something else. Like they're not in charge of their own money! Hmm, this wine just hits the spot!"

"You certainly need more room on the form if there's a chance that a beneficiary might be a minor and you want to name someone to be a Uniform Transfers to Minors Act custodian to hold the funds for the minor," commented Ben. "Or there could be any number of other reasons you'd want to take up more than two lines. I say, just write in 'See Attached,' and attach everything you need to."

"Yup. I've had success that way with some of the companies," said Rebecca.

Ben reminisced, "I remember one client who came to me when her original estate planning attorney retired. She thought everything was in good shape, but when we looked it all over, we found a problem. Her IRA beneficiary designation was to her two kids outright. But her Will had detailed instructions on how the assets going to Child B were to be managed. This kid was a spendthrift and would have spent it all in a year.

"So, I asked the client why all the instructions were there for Child B. She told me. Then, when we looked at her finances, we realized that the Probate estate passing under the Will was much smaller than the IRA and that she had some debts that would reduce it further.

"That meant that most of the money Child B would inherit was not going to be managed at all, because it was coming from the IRA!!!"

"Yikes," said Rebecca.

Over dessert, Ben commented, "I'm surprised by how little some of the customer service people, even professional money managers, understand about beneficiary designations at some of these major institutions. I remember, shortly before I retired, having a discussion with Andy over at Major Money Management Group. You know Andy—he's a high-level financial manager, very dedicated to providing good service, and he's been doing this for a long time. And MMMG is a respected outfit. But even Andy did not know that an estate or a charity could not be a 'Designated Beneficiary' of a qualified retirement plan or IRA."

Rebecca spoke up. "I was talking to Andy just today, and he told me about this very conversation. Andy now realizes that an IRA owner can give a charity a dollar amount, but not a percentage, without messing up the distributions to humans, or requiring splitting the IRA into two. As long as the IRA can pay the dollar amount within a legally set period after death and get the charity out of the picture, the other beneficiaries can have a little longer to take their money out."

Ben commented, "It's a shame that Congress just eliminated the lifetime stretch-out payment for many potential beneficiaries, but a ten-year payout is still better than having to take the money immediately and paying the tax. Still, under the new law, you have to deal with Eligible Designated Beneficiaries, Other Designated Beneficiaries, whatever. What a mess. I'm glad to be retired, Bec."

"Yes, there's always something new to learn," said Rebecca. "Did you know that the ten-year 'payout' law doesn't require you to withdraw money annually? You can let the account grow for ten years. And there's talk that the regulations, which aren't written yet, since the law is so new, might allow a beneficiary to keep the money in an inherited IRA until December 31 of the year in which the tenth anniversary of the death happens, so it would really be longer than ten years. This is one of those areas where professional advice is needed, Ben, and I'm doing my best to spread the word. More coffee?"

PORCH MUSINGS ON BENEFICIARY DESIGNATIONS

Ben and Roger were back on the porch, enjoying some fine Fall weather over a Diet Coke. Marianne and Louise, their wives, had weighed in on how the exercise they were doing was not sufficient to counteract the beer calories they had been taking in.

They were finishing a conversation about insurance beneficiary designations.

Roger commented, "You once told me that it was possible to leave my insurance to my estate, but I shouldn't do that with my IRA. What's that all about?"

"Well, with insurance, you might do that to give the estate some liquidity to pay your bills, and so on. Once the money is in the hands of the PR, it's available to pay bills. I'm not necessarily recommending that, but there's a lot of flexibility with insurance, because you don't have to think about taxation.

"There's special tax treatment with IRAs, so there are other considerations. For example, if you leave your IRA to your estate, the estate will collect it and pay the tax immediately. Most people want to extend the period of payment to delay the taxation."

Roger ventured, "I would guess that an IRA for a married guy like me would just go to my wife? Don't retirement benefits automatically go to the spouse?"

"Well, yes and no," said Ben. "There's a 1984 law that says you need to leave your retirement plan to your spouse, unless the spouse waives that right in conformity with particular technical requirements. But that applies only to a 'qualified' retirement plan. And the surprise here is that an IRA is not a 'qualified plan.'"

"It's not? But an IRA grows free of tax, and you have to start taking your required minimum distribution the same as with a pension plan!" exclaimed Roger.

"Right, you have to start taking it by April 1 of the year after the year you reach age 72. That deadline used to be April 1 of the year after the year you turn age 70½. But the 1984 law treats an IRA differently for purposes of spousal protection. If anyone thinks they don't need to worry about checking their IRA beneficiary designation because the spouse will get it anyway, they're just wrong.

"It also means that someone retiring from a company with a regular qualified retirement plan can thwart the spouse by putting the assets into an IRA with some beneficiary other than the spouse," said Ben.

"Live and learn. Enough of this. You're giving me a headache."

CHAPTER
FIVE

REVOCABLE TRUSTS

How do you set up a Revocable, or Living, Trust? Are Revocable Trusts really "Will substitutes"? Are they like super powers of attorney? How do you change the terms of a Revocable Trust?

BRAD AND JANE CONSIDER REVOCABLE TRUSTS

So much legal wisdom emerged over beer after the 18th hole that Jane was not surprised when her orthopedist husband came home from golf with a tidbit about which Brad was quite excited.

"Well, Jane—Jinx and I got to talking about our estate planning. I mentioned that we had not updated our estate plan for more than ten years, and he was kind of shocked when I told him we had Wills and no Revocable Trusts. According to him, the tax situation has changed, and his lawyer told him he had to have a Trust. Naturally, he was happy to tell me all about how he has the best, and if we don't have the same, we're going to pay a lot more tax than we need to."

"Yeah, I know, Brad—Jinx *always* has the best. But sometimes I think his breadth is greater than his depth, if you know what I mean. What made you get interested?"

"I guess the idea that we could avoid Probate and save a bunch of taxes."

Jane said, "Well, I'll believe it when I see it. Do you think we should check with Rebecca about whether we need an update? I could drop her an email and set up an appointment."

Rebecca Dalton had been practicing T&E law for 23 years, and Brad and Jane had been her clients for more than 15 of those. She knew their children's names and ages, strengths and weaknesses, the state of their marriage and their health, and the family long-term goals—all kids through college, comfortable retirement in North Carolina, two reasonably long vacations a year before then. And, clearly, she knew all about Brad and Jane's financial situation. Twice in the prior six years, they had called her to get information they had forgotten about their own finances.

A week later, in Rebecca's office, Brad asked her whether any changes were needed in their estate plan. "Well," she said, "I looked at your file this morning. I do think you should update your powers of attorney, both for finances and for health care. It's good to update them every few years. Also, some recent state-law changes should be reflected. Your Wills look fine, unless you know of some changes you want to make to them."

"Uh, OK, Rebecca. We're happy with updating the POAs. But I was kind of wondering about Trusts. Do we need Trusts?" asked Brad.

"Well, you know you do have Trusts in your Wills for your children, if needed. What kind of Trusts do you have in mind?"

"Well, my buddy was telling me recently that he and his wife have Trusts to save taxes and avoid Probate, and he said his lawyer sets them up for all of his clients," said Brad.

"OK, he's probably referring to what is called a 'Revocable Trust' or 'Living Trust.' This is a kind of alter ego that owns your assets. After you have the Trust document prepared and transfer ownership of your assets to the Trust, you are no longer the legal title owner, but you are still the beneficial owner. And since you are not the legal title owner, your death does not directly impact the legal title."

"Baby steps, Rebecca. If I do this Trust, I'm not the legal owner of my assets?" asked Brad.

"Right, but you are still the beneficial owner. You control what can happen with your assets. And you have the right to take all the assets back into your individual name if you want to. Assuming you have mental capacity!" she winked.

"You avoid Probate with a Trust like this because there is no asset in the actual name of the decedent. The Probate process deals with assets in the individual name of a decedent, and appoints the person who is qualified to take over those assets in place of the decedent."

"OK, so the Trust would have my assets, and I would be destitute. So, there would be no need for Probate when I died because I would be penniless. Do I have that right?"

She laughed. "Perhaps you're being just a little dramatic, Brad?!" They had known each other for years. Jane was smiling, too.

"As I said, the Trust is revocable. That means you can modify it or eliminate it by taking all of your assets back into your own name. But let's say you don't do that. The Trustee manages your assets while you are alive. The goals of the Trust while you are alive are to take care of you and Jane."

Brad stopped her again. "You mean I have to pay some Trustee to manage my own money?!?!? This is sounding worse and worse. I don't know why Jinx would want to do this or why he'd recommend it to anyone else."

"OK. Well, let me explain a little more. Here's how you set it up: You, as an individual, make a written agreement with yourself as Trustee. In this agreement, you, as Trustee, promise to manage the money and other assets that you, as an individual, give to yourself as Trustee for described purposes. Obviously, you don't have to pay yourself as Trustee."

"Wait," said Brad, again. "What do you mean that I 'give the assets to myself' as Trustee?"

"What I mean is that—and this happens only after you have a written Trust document—you actually change the name on your bank accounts, real estate, and so on to say that you now own those in your capacity as Trustee. So, for example, you close a bank account you have in the name 'Brad Baldwin' and open a new one in the name 'Brad Baldwin, Trustee of the Brad Baldwin Revocable Trust dated X,' where 'X' is whatever date you sign the Trust Agreement," answered Rebecca. "And you do that with any asset in your individual name."

"Then," she continued, "you, as Trustee, follow the written directions you included in your Trust agreement. It's an 'agreement' between you as an individual and you as Trustee. Legally, those are two different people. Sometimes the term 'declaration of Trust' is used when it's just the one person declaring that he is acting as Trustee of a bunch of assets for himself. Naturally, since it's all under your control, you can modify those written directions any time you want, as long as you have your mental capacity."

"Wow. That sounds kind of involved. Not sure I like the sound of this, but, OK. Assume I set up a Trust. What about Jane's assets?" asked Brad.

"Yes. Well, Jane would have her own separate Trust, with her own separate assets, to keep things clear as to who has the power to change how these things are managed. Right now, the two of you have minimal separately owned assets—most of them are joint—but when one of you dies, the survivor will become the only owner of all of your joint assets. So, at that point, he or she would move those assets into his or her Revocable Trust. There are other options, but let's assume that's how we would do it."

"OK—you're ahead of me again. Let's say I'm the Trustee, and I have a bunch of assets in my name as Trustee. What do I do with these assets? Anything I want?" asked Brad.

"Sure, pretty much anything. The Trust terms are set by you. The terms you would write into your Trust agreement would, in the usual case, allow expenditures for the grantor—that's you—and the grantor's spouse—Jane—first and foremost. Housing expenses, medical care, food, entertainment, travel. You know, since it's really your money—not as to legal title, but as to the use of it—you have flexibility. As long as you are alive and competent, you could be pretty loose, but you would need to spell out in the written Trust agreement how any successor Trustee could use your assets. I mean, if you give money to your kids regularly, you'd want to put it in writing that your successor can do the same. And you always name a successor Trustee in the document."

"What's a 'successor Trustee'?" asked Jane.

"The 'successor Trustee' is the person who would be in charge if you stopped being Trustee, which could happen through incapacity, death, or resignation," said Rebecca.

"Why would I resign?" asked Brad.

"You might resign because you no longer want to be bothered managing your finances, or you might think you're starting to lose your capacity." Rebecca chuckled. "I once heard of a completely competent woman who set up a Trust like this and named an independent Trustee from the start. She was wealthy and wanted a Trustee to manage her assets so she wouldn't have to bother. Her plan was to just keep going on cruises until she couldn't anymore."

Jane interjected, "Man, if I had that kind of money, I'd just get daily massages, hire a chauffeur and a chef. . . ."

Brad looked askance.

Rebecca asked if Brad and Jane would like more coffee. The meeting seemed to be stretching on. Then she resumed:

"There are two other aspects of Revocable Trusts you should understand. One is that the language in the Trust acts as your Will when you are gone. It will spell out the distribution plan you have, just as your existing Will does now. Since the successor Trustee already has control of the assets, he or she just follows the instructions you have laid out, and Bob's your uncle."

Rebecca continued, "The other thing about a Revocable Trust is that it acts like a super power of attorney. If you resign or can't keep managing your finances, the successor Trustee takes over. What *that* means, as far as drafting the document, is that everything you would want to do or have someone else do with your money during your lifetime would be spelled out, especially if it means using the money for someone other than yourself, like your kids or, maybe, a charity.

"As with a power of attorney, you can modify this whenever you want, as long as you have the mental capacity to do so. You can totally rewrite the terms, or you can make an amendment that modifies only part of the Trust document."

"So, there would also be provisions in this document that would be like what I have now in my Will, for when I die? Like, giving it to Jane if she survives me, and if she doesn't, one-third to each child, and so on?" asked Brad.

"Yes, a Revocable Trust can have any provisions a Will might have. So, the Revocable Trust is like a power of attorney substitute AND a Will substitute."

"Well, that sounds pretty good, Rebecca. Is there any real reason NOT to have a Revocable Trust?" asked Jane.

"Oh, no—not at all. For one thing, you never know when you might lose your capacity, in this uncertain world. You could have a stroke, be in an accident, be hit by lightning, fall off your skateboard . . . you know.

"It's not all that hard to set up a Trust, or two Trusts. We would draft a Trust for each of you, using the plan of disposition each of you has in your current Will as a model, and incorporating any changes you have thought about in the last ten years. And then we would retitle your assets out of your individual name into the name of the Trustee. This involves quite a lot of paperwork, as you can imagine."

"Then we toss our Wills?" Brad asked.

"Yes, you toss the existing Wills, but after the Trust is signed, you would sign a new 'pour-over' Will."

"A 'pour-over' Will?" asked Brad.

"That's a Will that picks up any assets you might have failed to move into the Trust," said Rebecca, before Brad interrupted her again.

"'Picks up'??? Please explain, Rebecca!" said Brad.

"Sure! So, the terms of the Trust instruct the Trustee—really, the successor Trustee—as to what to do with the Trust assets when you die. But if you die owning any assets in your individual name—maybe a stock certificate you had forgotten about, for example—the Trustee has no power over that asset. The only way someone can take control of that asset in your individual name after you die is to go to Court and have a person appointed to take charge. That's Probate. And the PR who is appointed would be directed in the pour-over Will to transfer any Probate assets to the Revocable Trust, to be managed under the plan set out in the Trust document."

Jane and Brad groaned. "This is all so new to us!"

"I know, it's a little foreign to think about giving away assets without really giving them away. Revocable Trusts are not for everyone. There is more complexity than some people want to take on. There is also a definite expense involved in setting them up.

"And the fact is, there is almost always some asset or other that, for any number of reasons, does not get transferred into the Trust. And the Trust document, of course, is where all of the distribution instructions are. So, for that reason, we always have the client sign a Will that controls such assets and instructs the PR to move those assets under the Trust umbrella. Then they DO get controlled by the provisions of your Trust document."

"What if you don't need this pour-over Will, because when you die, everything is already in the Trust?" asked Jane.

"No problem. If you have no Probate assets, the Will is just a few pieces of unnecessary paper, but in my experience, there is almost always some individually-owned asset not in the Trust at death. For example, a tax refund that arrives too late to be added to the Trust assets, or even an asset that you couldn't transfer into the Trust, like a cooperative apartment, where the rules of the co-op prohibit such a transfer. Are you both with me?"

Jane and Brad nodded, both looking a little anxious.

Rebecca went on. "We would also rewrite your power of attorney to make it fit in with your Trust. The POA would allow your agent to add to the Trust any assets the agent runs across that are still in your individual name. So, you would each end up with a Trust, a Will, a power of attorney, and an advance medical directive."

"OK," Brad sighed. "I think I get it. Now, tell us about the tax savings. My friend Jinx said his Trust is saving him a lot of tax."

"Well, there, I have to say, he is a little confused. If he's talking about a standard Revocable Trust, it is basically invisible for tax purposes. The tax-identification number under which the Trust reports its income is your social security number, so there's no tax savings there. And when you die, since all of the assets were under your control, based on your power to revoke the trust and take back all the assets, they are counted as belonging to you for purposes of estate tax. Not that estate taxes are much concern to most people now that the tax threshold is so high—more than $11.58 million per person for federal estate tax."

"So, there's no tax savings at all??!!" exclaimed Brad.

"That's right. There are some tax-beneficial provisions you can put into a Trust document, but they are exactly the same as what you could put into a Will. It's not because they are in a Trust that they save tax. Similarly, there are management provisions you can put into a Trust that could also be in a Will. So, if Jinx is saving taxes, the reason is that there are tax provisions in his Trust that could equally well have been in a Will."

"OK," said Brad. "Knowing Jinx and knowing you, I believe you!"

Jane asked "I just thought about something: if my bank account is in my name as Trustee of my Trust, do I need to sign every single check as 'Jane Baldwin, Trustee of the Jane Baldwin Revocable Trust, dated whatever'?"

"Well, that's one way to go, but there are a couple of ways around this—you and Brad could keep a joint account in your names and use that for most of your purchases, or you could have your Trustee title printed on the face of the checks, so that you just have to sign your name, or you could have a small account in your individual name. Even if that account would go through Probate at your death, it would likely be small enough to qualify for a special, abbreviated procedure.

"Setting up a Trust does involve a fair amount of paperwork in addition to the written document. I'll email you my explanation on how to transfer ownership of different kinds of assets into a Revocable Trust. Do you have any other questions?" asked Rebecca.

"No, I think that's it for now. Thanks, Rebecca," said Brad. "Jane and I will talk about this and call you in a few days."

MURPHY WANTS A TRUST

"Hi, Rebecca. It's nice to meet you," said Murphy Koslowitz, as he took a seat in Rebecca Dalton's conference room.

"And nice to meet you, too. I understand that Brad and Jane sent you to me?"

"Yes. I guess they saw you last week, and a few things they told me about that visit resonated. I recently learned that I am in the beginning stages of a degenerative disease."

"Oh, I'm sorry to hear that!" commented Rebecca.

"Thanks. Well, I just want to get my ducks in a row. From what Brad told me, there might be a few reasons I would want to have a Revocable Trust."

"OK. Well, I'm ready to hear them. What reasons do you have in mind?"

"First, the progression of the disease. It's in the early stages, and the doctors are hopeful, and it's mostly physical, not affecting cognition. But still, I may run out of energy to manage my own assets, and I'm pushing 70 right now.

"Second, I own a lot of parcels of real estate, and they are kind of dispersed. I own property in four states and the District of Columbia."

"Well, that's quite a widespread empire, then! And I guess Brad told you that you would need an ancillary Probate in every one of those jurisdictions if you died owning the properties in your own name."

"Yes, that's what got my attention. Here's a list of my properties," he said, handing over his spreadsheet.

Rebecca reviewed the list. "Well, there's one place that might not require an ancillary Probate: this unit in Asheville, North Carolina. I see that it's in a cooperative apartment building. When you have a co-op, you might be deemed not to have real estate in the state. The paperwork allows you to occupy a certain piece of real estate, but it's more like owning stock than owning a piece of land, so, in some states, it's treated for Probate purposes as if you own stock, and a Probate might not be required locally. I don't know about North Carolina.

"We can try to transfer all of these properties into a Revocable Trust, but some co-ops have rules against that. There's no problem with the condominiums and the other parcels of real estate."

"OK," said Murphy. "I guess you'll have to talk to lawyers in all of these jurisdictions, to deed the properties over to my Trust."

"Right!" said Rebecca. "It's a lot of paperwork, and we will hire a local attorney for some of these transfers, because doing a deed can be considered the practice of law, and I'm not licensed in all of these places. But still, there's less paperwork than there would be if these properties had to go through multiple Probates at the time of your death."

"Obviously, the other thing that is pushing this now is the idea that the Trust is like a super power of attorney. How does that work?" asked Murphy.

"Well, let's say you are the initial Trustee for yourself—you're single?"

"Yes."

"OK. Well, the Trust document will state that the Trustee can take care of you and any other people you ordinarily care for, if there are any. While you're the Trustee, you really have a lot of flexibility, but the rules are written down for whoever takes over if you lose your capacity. Or resign."

"That's my brother, Riley."

Rebecca's eyebrows went up. "Riley Koslowitz?!?"

"Yeah," he chuckled. "Our mother was Irish."

"Aha! Well, Riley would give proof of his Trusteeship to the various institutions where the Trust assets are held, and he would be able to use your assets to take care of you. He'd pay your—the Trust's—real estate taxes, for example, and also make sure your needs are paid for—medical care, household management, entertainment, payment of any other regular bills. He'd make sure your pets are cared for, if you have any. He would preserve your assets, file tax returns for you, continue making charitable contributions, but only if, and to the extent that, they were specifically authorized in writing.

"We'll talk about the specific provisions next, but I'm glad to know you're prepared for the paperwork. Setting up the Trust properly is a lot of work now, but it saves a bunch of time and effort when you die."

"I know, and I guess it's more private than Probate, too. Oh—one more thing: if I want to change the terms of the Trust, do I just do a Codicil?"

"Yes, it's definitely more private," confirmed Rebecca, "and, no, you don't do a Codicil. It's called an 'amendment.' And, of course, you can change anything you want. You can even remove yourself as Trustee, but, of course, you could just resign, too. You could change the Trustee powers; you could change ages for distribution; you could change beneficiaries. You always retain the power to amend it further, as long as you have the mental capacity."

"OK. I think that's all I need to know about that. Let's start on the terms of my Trust!"

MARK LEARNS ABOUT REVOCABLE TRUSTS

". . . Anyway, I learned something out of all of this," Mark commented to Terry as they sat over coffee in her living room.

"I always thought that, if you had a Revocable Trust, you didn't have to go through Probate."

"Well, yeah. Isn't that the point of having a Revocable Trust—that you don't have to go through Probate?" asked Terry.

"Hah! Yes, but you have to set it up right. First, you get your Trust document lined up, you sign it, and your Trustee signs to accept the job. Then, after that's done, you have to actually change the ownership of your assets into the name of the Trustee. So, my Aunt Lois didn't take that second step."

"Not sure what you're saying, Mark."

"What I'm saying is that my Aunt Lois had a Trust document all neatly drawn up by her attorney, Rebecca Dalton, and told me that she was naming me to take over as Trustee at her death—or if she became incapacitated. And Rebecca explained to my aunt that she needed to change title to her assets, to 'fund' the Trust."

"'Fund'?"

"Yes, that means to transfer stuff into it. She offered to have the paralegals in the office help Lois, but Lois wanted to save money and said she'd do it herself. Rebecca gave her a long form explaining how to do it, but now we learn that Lois did not follow through. Without taking this step, to actually put the assets in the name of the Trustee of the Trust, the Trustee had control of nothing. So, when Lois died, I had control of nothing at all, because nothing was in the Trust except the $10 she contributed to it when she set it up in Rebecca's office."

"No kidding! What happens now?"

"Well, those assets go through Probate now! Rebecca told me Probate is not such a big bugaboo, but it seems like unnecessary work to set up a Trust and then not make full use of it."

"More coffee, Mark? So, how does this work?"

"Sure, two sugars, please. Fortunately, Lois had a 'pour-over' Will. This 'pour-over' Will, of which I'm the Personal Representative, gives me control of any Probate assets she might have—which, in Lois's case, is basically everything she owned!—and directs me to change the ownership from Lois's name to my name as Trustee. So we're OK. The Trust will still control where everything ends up."

"Well," said Terry, "it sounds like a lot of trouble to change all these ownerships. I mean, I have a brokerage account, three bank accounts, an IRA, a house, a car, some art work, my household furnishings, some life insurance. If I set up a Revocable Trust, would I have to transfer all this stuff?"

"From what I understand, now that I have been talking to my aunt's lawyer about this, you can transfer stuff that is not actually registered anywhere—like normal furnishings of your house—by a paper 'declaring' it to be in your Trust. And when I say 'in your Trust,' I mean in the name of the Trustee. So, there would be a page in the Trust document 'declaring' that all of the contents of the house are assets of the Trust, held by the Trustee.

"But this 'declaration' thing does not work for anything where your name is on record somewhere naming you as the owner, like the bank accounts or even a really valuable artwork, or, more commonly, a car or other vehicle."

"This all makes me wonder if it's worth having a Trust," mused Terry. "Thinking of myself, I guess I could see doing the deed and the paperwork for the bank accounts and IRA and insurance, depending on how bad Probate is."

"Oh, no," noted Mark. "You wouldn't put an IRA or your insurance in the name of the Trustee because these things are governed by contracts with some financial institution. The contract terms are: you ask some financial institution to manage it, and they agree that, when you die, they will give what is left to the person you named in your beneficiary designation."

"Huh?"

"Well, your IRA and insurance go to your named beneficiaries without going through Probate. If you are trying to avoid Probate, you need only to be sure you have signed beneficiary designations for your retirement accounts and life insurance. But you would take anything you own in your individual name and retitle it into a Revocable Trust."

"So, this is all very interesting. It's amazing how vague I am on these things. I remember your Aunt Lois. It's kind of surprising she didn't follow through on all of this. And why didn't the lawyer just make sure she made these changes?"

"I guess a lawyer can't really force someone to incur another legal bill, and apparently Aunt Lois thought she could do it herself with the instructions the lawyer gave her. She probably thought she had already paid enough to have the Will and Trust documents done."

"I suppose it's none of my business, but what would have happened if she had not done the Will?"

"Hah! It would have been a *disaster*! If Aunt Lois had not done the pour-over Will, the Trust would have been completely useless. If she had had no Will, and just this Trust with only $10 transferred to it, the trust would pay out the $10 as stated in the trust. All the rest of Aunt Lois's assets would have passed by the law of intestate succession to my Uncle Bob—that's Aunt Lois's brother—plus my mother—that's Lois's sister—and my cousins Ralph and Georgia, who are the children of my Mom's other sister, who died about five years ago. That's just not what she wanted.

"So, although there will be a bigger Probate than she would have expected, her wishes will be followed, leaving some of her money to friends, and some to a few charities, and the rest to family. The pour-over Will ensures that her plan will still be carried out. Good coffee, by the way! Thanks."

LURLEEN BECOMES INCAPACITATED

Caroline was talking to Frieda before book club about an earlier conversation with Lurleen: "Caroline, I have named you to take over my affairs 'if I lose it.' That's what she told me a few years ago, but I never thought it would happen," commented Caroline.

"How did you find out you were going to need to step up?" asked Frieda.

"I got a call from Lurleen's neighbor last week. This neighbor, Pat, happened to see Lurleen collapsed in her backyard and called an ambulance. Lurleen had told Pat about me, so she got in touch with me. It's tough for older people living alone.

"Anyway, when Pat called me, I went over to Massive Medical Center with my medical power of attorney, and the doctors told me Lurleen had had a severe stroke. It took a few days to see what kind of recovery she was going to have, but she hasn't made much progress."

"Man, I'm sorry to hear this—both because I always liked Lurleen but also because I know it will be a lot of work for you."

"I know. But Lurleen had a Revocable Trust, and she had properly changed all of her assets into her name as Trustee, with me as a backup. I talked to her lawyer, and she is guiding me in the process.

"I just need to look at Lurleen's records of what is in the Trust and let the various institutions know that I will now be signing checks and buy-sell orders, and so on. And I have to find out what bills she has and make sure I pay them on time. I sure hope I won't need to sell her house," Caroline mused. "But if Lurleen is never able to come home, I'll have to deal with the house. And its contents. Whew."

"Is it really just a matter of showing these various banks that the document names you to be the successor Trustee? Couldn't Lurleen have written a later document naming someone else?" asked Frieda.

"Well, yes—she could have! Her lawyer was not aware of any later change. There is some trust involved here. No pun intended. I mean Lurleen told me I would be in charge. She told the neighbor to call me, and I called Lurleen's lawyer to see what I was supposed to do. The lawyer doesn't believe Lurleen made any changes removing me, and nobody else has stepped forward. But, in theory, Lurleen could have changed all of this—she could change the Trust any time she wanted."

"Not now," commented Frieda wryly.

"Right, not now."

A month later Frieda called Caroline. "Well, Caroline, how are things going with Lurleen's Trust? Have you been able to take over? And I'm really sorry to hear that Lurleen is not doing better."

"It was pretty easy to get control of the assets. In the end, Lurleen's banks asked me to certify in writing that I was the actual successor Trustee. This protects the banks and would expose me to liability if I lied. So, the hard part is managing her care and facing the sale of her house.

"But I have to say, now that it looks like Lurleen is never coming back, I'm really sad. I miss her."

PART TWO

Other Planning Arrangements

CHAPTER
SIX

GIFTS

Can gifts cause problems in the family? How do you know when a transfer is really a gift? What tax effects of a gift should I understand?

YULIA'S CONSEQUENTIAL GIFT

Yulia Vronsky died a widow. In the course of sorting through their mother's papers, Marcella and Trevor Vronsky learned that, a year before she died, their mother signed a deed transferring her farm to them. At their initial meeting with Rebecca Dalton to discuss the estate administration, they brought the new deed to her attention.

Trevor commented: "Mom saved us a lot of trouble, because we plan to sell the farm after we empty the house and barn. And since it's now in our names, we're free to go ahead. We've been told it's worth about $1.5 million."

Rebecca looked at the deed and groaned.

"Um, Rebecca," asked Marcella, "why did you make that kind of groaning sound?"

"Well, I'll get to that—let me ask for a little background. Do you happen to know how much your mother paid for the farm?"

"I think our folks paid about $300,000, but that was a long time ago," commented Trevor.

"You have told me the farm is now worth around $1,500,000. What do you think it was worth when your dad died?" asked Rebecca.

"I think, when Dad died, it was listed on his papers as being worth $900,000, right Marcy?" said Trevor. Marcy nodded.

"OK. I hope you two are math geeks. I groaned because there is a bad tax effect of this deed. This takes some arithmetic, so stick with me.

"Let's use $300,000 as a starting number, because you think that is what your parents paid when they bought the property. For purposes of this exercise, assume your parents put $100,000 into improvements. And then let's assume it was all worth $900,000 when your father died. Do you know what the term 'tax basis' refers to?"

"Umm, maybe you could refresh us," Marcy said.

"Sure. It's the calculation you use when you sell an asset to determine how much of the sales proceeds are to be taxed as capital gain. Roughly, what you paid for the asset, plus the cost of improvements you have made, is your 'tax basis' in that asset. If you have depreciated it, the tax basis is reduced. The difference between this basis and what you sell the property for is capital gain. The capital gain at sale may also be reduced by some expenses of sale, but you get the idea.

"So, while your parents were alive, their tax basis in the property was, let's say $400,000, or $200,000 each, which I arrived at by adding the purchase price of $300,000 to the assumed $100,000 of improvements and dividing by two."

"OK—we're with you," said Trevor.

"Now, perhaps you are aware of the so-called 'adjustment' to tax basis that happens when someone dies. Each asset owned by a decedent takes as its new tax basis its value as of date of death. Some people call this a 'step-up,' but the basis goes *up* only if the asset is actually worth more at the time of death than they paid for it. Sometimes assets *lose* value, so I just call it a basis 'adjustment' instead of a 'step-up.'"

"OK, we're following," Marcy noted. Trevor nodded.

"All right. Here we go: When your father died, his half of the property got this basis adjustment. It was just automatic—nobody had to file for anything, and nobody will ever be taxed on the difference between the $200,000 tax basis he had in his half and the $450,000 that half was worth when he died. So, without any capital gains tax being paid on that $250,000 gain, his death added $250,000 to the overall tax basis in the property. If this were a community property state, the entire property would have received a tax basis adjustment, but that's not the case here.

"Naturally, you need supporting records, such as a then-current appraisal, to show that the basis adjustment numbers are right, if the I.R.S. questions them. I imagine you have something to show that the property was worth $900,000 when he died?"

"Yes, I'm pretty sure we do," affirmed Marcy and Trevor.

Rebecca continued, "That means that, after your father died, when the entire farm became your mother's by virtue of her surviving your father, her basis in the entire farm was the sum of her own basis in her half, $200,000, and his adjusted basis, $450,000, for a total of $650,000."

"OK, that's cool! So now we get another adjustment because of Mom's death?" Marcy asked.

"Ahem," started Rebecca. "No, I'm afraid not."

"OK, I'm not quite following," said Trevor. "But I have this weird premonition."

"Oooh, I *am* following," said Marcy. "This basis adjustment happens only if someone owns the property when they die. If I hear you right, Rebecca, you're saying Mom didn't own the farm when she died, because she gave it to us last year. That means there's no step-up, or adjustment, to her basis. Is that what you're saying??!!" Marcy's voice was rising.

"Um, yes. Unfortunately, that *is* what I'm saying. By means of this gift, your mother conveyed to the two of you her own tax basis in the property, $650,000. In a gift, the tax basis transfers over. Only in a transfer at death do you get a new adjusted basis.

"What that means is, if you sell the farm for its fair market value, which you think is about $1.5 million, you're going to have tax on your $850,000 capital gain," said Rebecca. "If, instead, you don't sell it and just keep it until you die, your beneficiaries will get an adjusted basis at that time."

"Well, isn't the exemption like $11 million now? We could sell without really worrying, couldn't we?" asked Trevor.

"Apples and oranges, Trev. The $11.58 million exemption you're thinking of is for another kind of tax. That is the exemption from federal estate tax on your mother's worldwide assets at death. That's a *transfer* tax. We are talking about part of *income tax* law here. The capital gain is taxed at a better rate than a lot of ordinary income, such as wages, would be—but the capital gains tax is part of the income tax system, and you don't have an exemption to protect you from that tax."

"And Mom could have avoided all of this if she hadn't transferred the farm to us!!??!! Bummer. Why would she do that?" asked Trevor.

"I wish I could tell you," said Rebecca. "Maybe she knew that would keep her farm out of Probate, which it does. And that saves a little bit of hassle, 'though not anywhere near enough to justify the tax. All I can say is that, sometimes, smart people have conversations with friends about how to set up their affairs, and they make changes that just don't work in their own situation."

"I think I need an adult beverage," said Marcy.

[*Note to reader: In community property states, or in a common law state whose law preserves the community property character of an asset brought from a community property state, as to such an asset, Dad's death would have given a basis adjustment to the entire property, and Mom's basis would have been $900,000.*]

CARRIE WETHERS AND THE AMBIGUITY

Carrie Wethers lived down the street from Ben Morgan. One morning, while walking her dog, she ran into Ben, picking up the paper. They exchanged pleasantries, and then Carrie asked Ben if she could bother him about something.

"Sure!" said Ben.

"OK, well—here's the thing," Carrie started, clearly a little uncomfortable. "My husband's father died a couple of years ago, and we have a kind of ongoing problem. My father-in-law helped Bob's brother, Carl, go to graduate school. Bob and I were already married. Carl was married too, with a young child. But Carl needed more education to get a better job, and he got admitted to business school."

Carrie continued, "Bob was a little frosted. Bob had worked his way through law school, paying the full freight himself, and here Dad is helping Carl. Bob thought Carl should have managed without money from Dad, like we did. But the expletive deleted really hit the fan when Bob's dad died."

"Ah, yes. The moment of truth," Ben commented.

"Well, what *was* the truth was the question. The records showed that Dad had supplied Carl with some $80,000. That's not insignificant in our family."

"I think I know what's coming," said Ben. "My guess is that nobody had specified if this was to be a loan or a gift."

"Yes! You hit the nail on the head," said Carrie. "Bob's dad had not filed gift tax returns, which would have indicated that the payments to Carl were intended as gifts. But he had not had Carl sign any promissory notes, either, which would have shown they were loans. Carl took the position that the payments were gifts, so he didn't owe the estate anything. Bob took the position that they were loans and said Carl should pay the money back.

The Executor went with Carl's position. And suddenly there's a rift in the family, and we can't have Thanksgiving with Carl and his family anymore," said Carrie, sadly.

"Well, I hope that will heal in time. This is such a common problem, and very few people think ahead to the moment you are in now. And, from a practical standpoint, depending on how long ago this transfer was made, the statute of limitations for collecting a debt may have expired.

Ben continued, "I know this isn't any help, but, speaking from experience, I can state categorically that any lack of clarification about stuff like this, while a niggling matter on a 'To Do' list during life, becomes a gigantic 'What Now?' after death. Any time a large amount of money is transferred within a family, the parties should look straight at it and record what their understanding and expectations are about what that transfer is. Is it an advancement on an inheritance, a gift, a loan to be repaid?"

"Wait," said Carrie. "What's an 'advancement'?"

"Oh, that's a gift that is considered as a sort of prepayment of an inheritance, or of part of an inheritance. You want to document a thing like that—even in the Will itself. Of course, you can also have a kid sign a promissory note for every big transfer, but that's a pain, and it's also a pain to file a gift tax return. But, as you have seen, the pain created after death from *not* settling this in life is hugely greater, when only one side is available to tell the story. And, frankly, it's possible that Dad himself had not decided whether he intended these transfers to be loans or gifts."

"I hear you," said Carrie. "But what do we do now?"

"There is no 'right' or 'wrong' now. Perhaps, over time, Carl and Bob will independently agree that their father did no favor to their relationship by sweeping this under the rug. Maybe Carl will decide he cares more about Bob than he does about the money and at least repay half. Maybe Bob will adjust to the inequality of it. I wish I could help more, but now it's up to time and recollection of once-happier days."

"OK," said Carrie. "I guess you're counseling us to be wiser than we have been. Thanks."

CHAPTER
SEVEN

MARITAL RIGHTS

Does getting married co-opt your estate plan? What about getting divorced? Are there ways to limit what you give your spouse? What are the drawbacks of joint ownership with a spouse?

FRED AND ANNIE SIGN A PRENUPTIAL AGREEMENT

Fred and Annie had been seeing each other long enough to decide they would be exclusive. No more thoughts of Match. com, no worrying about saying something that would innocently turn off a date; they had fun together and knew how to discuss, without rancor, any minor annoyance that might arise.

Except their future.

Fred had two children from his first, failed marriage. Annie had a son, too, by her late husband. At ages 47 and 45, Fred and Annie were not ready to give up on romance, but their children came first in their private lists of what counted the most.

And so, when Fred suggested marriage to Annie, she hesitated. "You know, Fred, it has been great being with you. I don't want this to end. Nobody else would have known I wanted to go kayaking on my birthday, or how much I love modern art, or would think to bring Johnnie a signed baseball, and so much more. Still, I just don't know about getting married."

"Well, is there something about me that gives you concern? I hesitate to ask, but I'll try to accommodate you, if I can."

"Oh, no! You are just about perfect for me, as far as I can tell. But you know I have an inheritance from when Bob died, and I think it's only right for it to go to Johnnie when I die—not to a new husband, no matter how wonderful he is!"

"Well, I could assure you that I would take care of Johnnie if you died before I did, but I'm not sure you'd be happy with that. And, of course, I want my kids to inherit from me, too. Let me call my lawyer and see what he recommends."

The next day Fred called his lawyer.

"Howard? This is Fred Jackson. I'm calling to see what you would recommend I do about my relationship with Annie Phelps. I've told you about her before. I'd like to marry her, but we want to protect our children financially."

"It's great that you called, Fred. Congratulations for having done the hard part—finding the right person! What you need is a prenuptial agreement, of course. In some states—including ours, you can even marry first and then make an agreement—then it's a 'postnuptial' agreement. A 'prenup' or 'postnup' is a contract between two parties to a marriage. Usually it deals with disposition of assets in event of death of the parties and also in event of divorce. But you have to do it right to make it stick, and I've seen it done wrong."

"Well, there won't be a divorce in our case! What do you mean, you've seen it done wrong?"

"So, sometimes the couple fails to recognize that they are negotiating with the other party to give up some rights each party has as a spouse. I mean, this is for real—they are on two sides, and they need two lawyers. They think they are on the same page, so they don't have to have a lawyer, or they can use the same lawyer. No lawyer I know would represent both parties in a prenup!"

"You're saying that the two parties have conflicting interests?" asked Fred.

"Exactly. A spouse, in every state in the union, has certain rights set out in state law to inherit from a deceased spouse. If someone dies with a spouse and with a Will that does not provide for the surviving spouse, the survivor can 'elect' to take against the Will. When that happens, the Will is ignored to the extent necessary to satisfy the legal rights of the survivor. I'm saying 'Will,' but, in some states, the rights go beyond just the assets that pass subject to the Will."

"Well, I don't feel like Annie and I are in conflict at all. We both want her assets to go to her son and mine to go to my children. And—I know we are lucky here—my kids really like her, and I know her son likes me."

"That will make it easier to design an agreement, then, but you still need to have two lawyers. This is to ensure that nobody is railroaded into an agreement. The lawyers' function is to make sure the clients understand what they are giving up. There's more."

"Yeeess??"

"You need to be forthright and open about all of your assets and liabilities. As ugly as it may sound, we are talking about rights to assets here. If you had $170 million, and Annie signed an agreement on the assumption she was giving up rights to her share of $1.7 million, she'd be righteously miffed if you died and left the whole thing to your kids, based on a misrepresentation by you. And she might be able to break the agreement after you died, assuming she survived you. So, each party is entitled to know the full financial situation of the other before signing an agreement. It's about fairness."

"Okay, so you're saying Annie and I need to have separate lawyers and we need to disclose our assets, liabilities, and, may I assume, income? Is there anything else?"

"Yes—income, too. Well, in a sense there is something else. Keep in mind the goal of fairness—this all has to do with whether the document would stand up in Court if it were challenged later. So, there's the issue of avoiding duress. In other words, asking your intended to sign a pre-nup the night before a 200-guest wedding with a seated dinner reception is a really bad idea. It will definitely weaken the enforceability of the agreement, if it's challenged. The longer the time before the actual wedding you can arrange to do this agreement, the better."

"Gee, it sounds so cold and formal."

"I know," said Howard. "But it's an act of love for your children. And, truthfully, if you and Annie are not on the same page as to your finances, it might be better to find out now—not years from now."

"Yeah, I guess you're right. I'll talk to her and get back to you."

"And Fred? Keep in mind that, as with any contract, you two can agree to change it later. Again, if you make changes, you want to make them only with complete knowledge of the implications, so each of you should, again, have your own competent lawyer, make full disclosure of finances, and so on. Finally—this is important—if you move out of state, you need to have the document reviewed to make sure its effect is not modified by state law. Good luck—and, I hope, congratulations!"

Fred reported back to Annie. "Annie—I talked to my lawyer. He says we can accomplish what we want with a prenuptial agreement. But there are certain requirements. One of them is that we each need to have a separate lawyer."

"Does he have another lawyer in his firm who could be my lawyer?"

"I don't think it works that way. If the firm is representing me, it can't represent you, too. But I could ask Howard to recommend someone for you. He said it's important that the lawyer be experienced in drafting prenups. So, could we have dinner tonight—maybe at La Maison des Pretensions? I want to ask you an Important Question."

Fred popped the question, and Annie and Fred were engaged. They pulled together their asset/liability lists. Fred was surprised to learn that Annie's husband had left her a Trust fund from which she received $100,000 per year, on top of her librarian salary of $55,000. He had also left a 401(k) plan that she had converted to an IRA in her own name. She also owned her house free and clear. Johnnie had student loans that Annie was helping to pay.

Annie learned that Fred's business made him a steady income of $180,000, so their incomes were almost identical. But he still had a mortgage and had just finished paying child support to his former wife. The kids were in college, and he needed to be careful about spending decisions.

Inasmuch as the children were mostly out of the house, Fred and Annie thought they could live together in her house and rent out his house for enough to cover the mortgage, taxes, and insurance. Negotiations ran smoothly. As Howard had suggested, they had the deal mostly worked out before they got the lawyers involved.

The lawyers—Howard and a qualified lawyer friend of his in another firm—met individually with their respective clients and asked them some questions relating to workability, suggesting how to manage the residence if Annie died first, since it was in her name. They talked about how to handle the beneficiary designation on Fred's 401(k) plan. Annie, as a spouse, would have a right to it unless she waived that right within a certain time frame. So, since they had to be married before she could sign a valid waiver, the waiver could not itself be part of the prenup—what a technicality!

In the end, Fred and Annie decided they wanted their children to be part of the process. So, they had a meeting in which the two lawyers, the two lovebirds, and the three children discussed the entire prenup. This is not something all parents would be interested in doing with their children, and the kids were appropriately appreciative to be treated as adults who could be trusted with such sensitive information.

Many years later, when Fred died, Howard's successor at the firm handled the estate administration. He had known of Howard's high regard for Fred and was not surprised to see that Fred had maintained the agreement properly.

Fred and Annie had held their assets as separate for the duration of their marriage, aside from a relatively small "operating" checking account and an emergency fund, both in joint names, which thus passed to the survivor. Theirs had been the perfect example of a prenuptial agreement done right.

PORCH MUSINGS ABOUT MARITAL RIGHTS

"Hey, Ben. Let's stop and rest a minute. If I didn't know better, I'd think you had been working out behind my back. I'm bushed. And I have a question."

"OK, Roger. Want some lemonade? A beer?"

They climbed the steps to Ben's porch, and Ben got each of them a beer. "What's your question?"

"So, I know that spouses have a special position in estate planning. I mean, you can't cut them out—I mean, I *think* I know that. It's true, right?"

"Well, yes, for the main part, but there are wrinkles."

"Hah! There are always 'wrinkles' in the law. Anyway, if you had a married guy who died, and his Will left everything to his cousin in Omaha, or maybe more realistically, his kids, ignoring the wife, what would happen?"

"OK. Plain vanilla? We are assuming they had *not* made a contract to waive their interests in each other's estates—by that, I mean a prenuptial agreement or a postnuptial agreement?"

"Yes."

"OK. In that situation, the wife has what is called a 'right of election' against the Will. The wife, within the time limit established by state law, files a paper in Court saying, essentially, 'I don't want the $100 my husband left me in his Will; I want my statutory elective share.' That is likely to be maybe one-third of the estate, maybe half. In some states, the wife's share depends on how long they have been married."

"And," said Roger, "that assumes the Will left $100 to the wife."

"Good catch, Rog. In some states, if the Will leaves nothing at all to the wife, the wife is *assumed* to have made the election, even without going to Court, and she collects the elective share, with no further ado. In that case, the Executor—we call that person a 'Personal Representative' now—has to carry out the law, and, perhaps, will need to be *reminded* to hand it over, by the wife or her attorney, but that is what the law provides, at least in some jurisdictions."

Roger asked, "Why is it so iffy whether it's a half or a third or some other percentage?"

"Well, all of this is controlled by state law, and states vary widely. Variables that affect the percentage could be: Were there children from the marriage? Did either spouse have children outside the marriage? And, as I mentioned, the length of the marriage may be a consideration. And then you have the whole issue of whether your state bases the calculation of the elective share on only the Probate assets or on some non-Probate assets, too."

"You mean, if I have most of my assets in a retirement plan, or life insurance, or joint property with my kids, I could cut Louise out entirely?" asked Roger.

"Well, that would work in some states!" noted Ben.

"But if they have a prenup, this does not happen," Roger presumed.

"Correct," said Ben, "but only if the Court knows about it. In my office, if there was a marital agreement like a prenup or postnup, we always mentioned it in the Will. An unscrupulous surviving spouse could 'forget' to mention that she had signed a prenuptial agreement waiving her rights.

"And, Rog," said Ben, warming to the topic, "as you suggested, this gets trickier than you might expect. If the decedent has no assets in the Probate estate—because nothing he owns is in his individual human name, like those assets you just described—the Will covers zippo. So, in many states, the right of election covers nothing at all, because the right applies only to assets passing through Probate, under the terms of the Will."

Ben continued, "Some states have figured this to be an unfair loophole, and have passed an 'augmented estate' law. This gives a spouse the right to claim a share in a broader category of assets, even, possibly, including assets the decedent has given away."

"Huh? How does that work?"

"Not easily! It's worked out in the calculation of the value counted in the base number on which the elective share is based, Roger. And there are credits. For example, in calculating the elective share in a state with an augmented estate law, joint property the surviving spouse owned with the decedent is credited against the share. It gets complicated, but this system pretty much ensures that the surviving spouse gets at least something—assuming there are assets somewhere."

Roger clarified, "OK, so a spouse can waive any interest in the other spouse's estate by some prenuptial agreement or even postnuptial agreement. Otherwise the surviving spouse has a legal right to part of what the deceased spouse owned. I get that. But what if everything they owned was in joint name?"

"Then nothing is waived by a prenuptial or postnuptial agreement. The joint property, or tenancy by the entirety property—that's only between spouses—just belongs to the surviving spouse by operation of law. It does not go through the Probate estate, is not subject to creditors' rights, and is not affected by the right of election."

"Say, Ben—how about another beer?" asked Roger.

Ben appeared with a second round of beer and a bag of nacho chips and settled back into his rocking chair.

"Thanks, pal. So, while you were inside, I realized I've always wondered what the deal is with community property—I keep hearing that term."

"Ah, yes," said Ben. "You know, we don't have that here. There are about nine states that have community property laws, and they're mostly in the West. Some common law states—those are non-community property ones, except for Louisiana, which has a unique system—will allow property to be held as community property if it was owned by spouses in a community property state, say, California, and they moved to, say, Virginia. Virginia is not a community property state, but it allows spouses who brought community property in from another state to continue to hold their community property assets in that form.

"Anyway, the big part of it for us here is that it affects the tax basis of a surviving spouse in the community property assets. You know what 'tax basis' is, right?"

"Yes, I think so. It's the amount on which you don't have to pay capital gains tax when you sell an appreciated asset. Like, if I bought a painting for $10,000 and sold it for $15,000, I would pay tax on the $5,000 over what I paid for it, but the $10,000 would be my 'basis' and not taxed. Right?"

"Right. Here's the thing about community property: If you and Louise owned that painting as community property and you died without selling the painting, Louise could sell it for $15,000 and have no capital gains tax to pay. The tax basis would adjust at your death to the painting's full fair market value at that time."

"Hmm. Well, what happens in these states that are common law states? Is there no adjustment to tax basis?" asked Roger.

"Yes, there is, but only for the part deemed to be owned by the deceased spouse. So, in the painting example, if you died owning half, that half gets an adjusted basis, but

Louise's half does not. Using the same example, you two buy a painting for $10,000, and you die when it's worth $15,000. Your half gets an adjusted basis of $7,500, but Louise's half still has a basis of $5,000. If she sells the painting for $15,000, she has a capital gain of $2,500. As I said, if you were in a community property state, there would be no capital gain."

"That's quite a benefit, all right!" said Roger.

THE DIVORCED PROCRASTINATOR'S WILL

"Hi, Rebecca. My cousin just died, and I'm in charge of administering his estate. I haven't the vaguest idea what's involved. Can we set up an appointment?"

Two days later, Phyllis Atwind was in Rebecca Dalton's office with her cousin's Will. "Here's the original Will. I guess you need that for the Probate?"

"Indeed, I do. Thanks. How did you happen to have it?" asked Rebecca.

"Well, Cal gave it to me when he got divorced. He figured I was the one who would need it if he ever died. 'If' he died. Funny how we say that."

"I know. I hear that all the time. OK, the Will says that Natasha Collins is the first named PR, with you as a backup. Did Natasha die?"

"No, she's alive and well. She's Cal's ex-wife. I guess I assumed she would be completely out of this."

"Hmm. I see the Will is 15 years old. When did they get divorced?"

"Maybe ten years ago. Maybe fewer. I'm not sure. Are you saying this Will is still effective? He leaves about half of his estate to Natasha!!!" exclaimed Phyllis.

"Nope, it's OK. In this state, you just treat the former spouse's share the way you would if she had died before he did. So, Natasha gets nothing from his Will, but the charities he has in this Will still get their bequests.

"I have to say, though, Cal's intentions could have been completely thwarted. If Cal had moved to DC, his divorce would have invalidated the entire Will. In Cal's state, it invalidates only the part of the Will providing for Natasha. This is one of those things that varies immensely from state to state."

"Oh, my goodness! That's crazy! And what about this insurance he left to her?" asked Phyllis.

"Do you know if the divorce settlement agreement mentions insurance? We'll look into all that, but if the settlement agreement says nothing about it, she might very well get it," said Rebecca.

"Hmph. I just hope we find out that he did a later beneficiary designation, giving the insurance to someone else. I don't really want to talk to Natasha after all these years.

"Just out of curiosity," asked Phyllis, "my husband and I have Revocable Trusts. We're not at all contemplating divorce, but what is the effect of divorce on provisions made for a spouse in a Revocable Trust?"

"Excellent question! Here is another area where state law varies a great deal. In some states, the Trust provisions for the former spouse are automatically invalidated by a divorce, and, in others—probably even more states—the former spouse still gets what is provided in the Trust. Fortunately, most divorce lawyers will urge their clients to revise their estate plans ASAP."

"But do they listen?" chuckled Phyllis.

THE REMARRIED CLIENTS

Rebecca was meeting with Craig and Betsy Newhart, happily married after prior divorces. Both spouses had children from their first marriages, and they wanted Rebecca to tell them what options they had for preserving assets for those children.

"It's great to meet you," said Rebecca, as they were sitting down. "I gather the Brookses gave you my name."

"Yes," said Craig. "We talked to them because they had been in our situation—prior marriages, prior kids. We want to provide for each other but also make sure our children get what's left when the surviving spouse dies."

"OK, then. Let's get right to it. You have a range of options. The most stringent, but effective, option, of course, would be a contract pertaining to disposition of the estate. I'm referring to a prenuptial agreement."

"Hah! Well, we can't be prenuptial, because we've been married eight years," noted Betsy.

"Not a problem," said Rebecca. "This state recognizes postnuptial agreements, too."

Rebecca explained the need for separate lawyers for each spouse, the need for full and fair disclosure of assets, liabilities, and income, the need for fairness in the signing of the document. They glanced at each other and asked Rebecca to move on to the next option.

"Well," said Rebecca, "if, with the postnuptial agreement you have a written agreement where the survivor gives up his or her rights to assets, at the other end of the spectrum, you have the full gift to the surviving spouse. A lot of spouses go this route, sometimes unintentionally, just by owning the bulk of their assets jointly with the spouse with right of survivorship."

"Oh, man!" exclaimed Craig. "You mean, if a couple puts all their assets into joint names with right of survivorship, and one dies, the survivor can do whatever the heck he or she wants with it??"

"Yes. That's exactly what I mean. There might be an understanding between the couple that, for example, the survivor will provide for the children of the predeceased spouse, but so many things can come up to prevent that from happening.

"For example, the children of the first-to-die spouse could, over time, lose contact with the survivor. And that might affect the loyalty of the surviving spouse to the plan made with the deceased spouse.

"Or, the survivor might marry again, become closer to another whole family of folks, and want to do something for them, reducing what is left for the children of the previous spouse."

Craig and Betsy were both looking disconcerted. "Well, what are some other options, then?" asked Betsy. "The 'give it all to the other' plan doesn't sound so good."

"I agree," said Rebecca. "The favored option in between these two extremes is a Trust for the surviving spouse."

"Oh, I have heard of these Trusts, and they save taxes, too!" exclaimed Craig.

"Well, if taxes are a concern to you—and we haven't yet looked at your finances—some of these Trusts can save taxes. But right now, I'm thinking about management, or control, of where the funds you own go after your death and the death of the spouse," said Rebecca.

"The basic model is a testamentary Trust in your Will for the surviving spouse. There is a Trustee, or possibly co-Trustees, with the surviving spouse being one of them. The purposes for which the Trustee or Trustees may distribute Trust funds are generally something like: 'All income to my wife, and distributions from principal for her support in reasonable comfort.'" Rebecca showed the air quotes.

"In a Trust of that sort, the wife—or the husband, if he is the surviving spouse—is assured of getting income. She can even be given a power to demand that the Trustee invest in assets that will produce a reasonable income. She is also assured of not starving, freezing, going without medical care, and so on. The standard guiding the Trustee's distributions for the surviving spouse is always limited in some way, such as 'support in reasonable comfort', since the goal is to be sure there is something left for children when the survivor dies.

"The Trust terminates at the survivor's death, and what remains after it is wound up goes to the beneficiaries named by the predeceased spouse. Are you with me?"

"I think so. I don't really know how Trusts work, but I think I understand that the Trust assets—which I suppose include money, stocks, real estate, or whatever the first dying spouse owned—all of this is sort of contained in a box under the control of the Trustee," said Craig.

Betsy asked, "What if the survivor wanted a bigger allowance or whatever? Could he or she just tell the Trustee to send it over?"

"No, it would not work that way. The Trustee is responsible to her—let's assume the survivor is a woman—but also to the children of the deceased husband, and perhaps to yet-unborn grandchildren, depending on the terms of the Trust. The Trustee would consider such a request and decide whether it was authorized by the document, taking into account applicable state law.

"You can see that it's important to make it as easy as possible for the Trustee to tell whether he's authorized to make any given expenditure. You spell out your goals and priorities in the document. Giving carte blanche would make the Trustee blanch, if I can be a little cute. The Trustee does not want that much discretion. The more guidance you can put in writing for the Trustee, the better. After all, the Trustee has to do his work without being able to consult you."

Betsy spoke again. "This is a little embarrassing to have to say, but Craig and I put everything in joint names when we got married. We thought it was just what married people do. And now I'm getting the idea that we might have been too hasty!"

"That's pretty common, but as you now know, that puts total control in the survivor's hands—or even in the hands of the people who might have influence over the survivor!

"We can separate the assets again, with a little paperwork. And we would have to do that, to ensure that there are assets passing under the Will into the Trust for the surviving spouse.

"But it's possible that you might decide to leave some things joint anyway. As we discuss your relative net worths and how much you want the children to get, you can make some specific decisions about all that," said Rebecca.

"Thanks, Rebecca," said Betsy and Craig together.

ASSETS FOR MINORS
AND OTHER YOUNG FOLK

How can you give assets to children who have no legal capacity to manage those assets? What options are there for managing the assets of children who are legal minors? What happens to life insurance left to a minor?

A BACKFIRED GIFT TO CHILDREN

". . . And, Janine, can you believe he left a $30,000 insurance policy to the kids, so they would have something directly from him? I just can't get over how sweet that is."

Kathy was still reeling from the death of her 38-year-old husband while jogging two days earlier. As her best friend, Janine was helping her organize the funeral. It was hard.

"Wow. That is really thoughtful," Janine agreed.

A few days later, Kathy and Janine met with the lawyer about winding up Ian's affairs. What a thought—winding up affairs of a 38-year-old. Nevertheless, it had to be done. They gathered all of Ian's financial records they could find and took them to the meeting.

Rebecca Dalton made the two ladies comfortable in the conference room and looked through the papers and the Will. The Will left everything to Kathy. It provided that, if Kathy did not survive Ian by 30 days, the assets would go to the children equally, with a Trust to hold the assets of each child under age 25. To Janine's surprise, she was named to be the Trustee for each of these Trusts. She vaguely recalled talking to Ian about this. The children were five, seven, and nine years old, so, if Kathy died in the next three weeks, there would definitely be Trusts, and they would last for some time! Janine told Kathy she expected her to survive. That got a weak smile.

"Ah," said Rebecca when she looked at the beneficiary designation on the insurance policy.

"'Ah,' what?" they asked at the same time.

"Ah, we have a small complication," said Rebecca.

"Small complication" did not sound like something they wanted to hear.

"Your children are minors, Kathy. So, they can't accept this insurance personally. That is the complication. The insurance company will not hand over assets to a child younger than 18. That does not mean the kids won't get the money, but it does mean their interests are protected by the Court until the children are 18," she explained.

"What do you mean, 'protected by the Court'?" Kathy asked.

"Well, it's kind of onerous. The Court names a guardian of the money. The guardian can be you, or it can be a friend or other family member."

"Well, why wouldn't it be me? I'm their mother!"

"It most likely would be you. But, in fact, the Court starts from scratch. Theoretically, anyone can apply to be the guardian," said Rebecca.

"In your case, I know of no reason that the Court would not appoint you. Still, you have to submit to the Court procedure, to satisfy the insurance company. The company knows that the stringent Court requirements will protect the company from some charge that it didn't care properly for the minor's money. No insurer wants to be sued by a kid who has just turned 18 years of age, complaining that the insurance company recklessly turned over his insurance money to an adult just because that adult was his parent. The parent—not you, but some—could be irresponsible. Alternatively, the insurance company could just hold the assets until your children reach age 18."

"Well, why not just put the insurance money into the Trust, like it says in Ian's Will? It looks like the Trustee has a lot of flexibility in managing the money for the benefit of the kids," Janine suggested.

"I wish it were that easy, Janine, but the insurance company has to follow the beneficiary designation, and this one does not leave the insurance to the Trusts under the Will. It just says to pay the money to the children."

"Oh, boy. Well, walk us through the steps, then," Kathy requested. Janine took notes.

"All right. There are several steps for setting up a Court-supervised guardianship of a minor. First, you file a petition with the Court to name an adult—in this case, you, Kathy—to be the guardian for each child. One petition can be used to set up the three guardianships; you don't need to do this three times."

"Thank goodness for small mercies," Janine muttered.

"In the petition, you need to give some information about your own finances, Kathy. The Court wants to know if you have adequate funds to raise the children without using these insurance proceeds, since that money belongs to the kids. The petition also gives enough information about you to reassure the bonding company that you will not abscond with the funds."

"What!!??"

"I'm sorry—that was a little direct. But the Court will not allow you to be appointed as guardian or to accept any funds unless you can qualify for a bond—like an insurance policy for the protection of the money."

"We're talking $30,000 here—it's not like protecting Fort Knox," Janine protested.

"I know. And, again, you could just leave the money with the insurance company, but most likely, you will want to control it, and they don't really want to keep it, anyway.

"So," Rebecca continued, "after you have filed all the information the petition for guardianship requires, the Court approves your appointment and assigns case numbers. Three separate guardianships are set up, one for each child, each with its own Court number.

"The appointed guardian—you—develops an investment plan for each guardianship—here, since we're talking about only $10,000 for each child, it can be simple, like investment in a couple of mutual funds for each guardianship."

"Can we get back to the bonding requirement, for a minute?" asked Kathy. "Are you saying that sometimes the parent is not able to get a bond?!!!?"

"That's right. This is not always a slam dunk. When an inexperienced guardian applies for a bond—I mean a young parent with little financial-management skill or who has a lot of creditors—the bonding company may not agree to write a bond. It's their ass on the line, excuse my French. So, they might not want to sell a bond without some guarantee, like an attorney as a co-guardian. But, in your case, you have plenty of assets of your own—well in excess of this $30,000—and there won't be any problem. Plus, you work in a bank, for heaven's sakes."

"OK."

"So, next, when the Court has appointed you, the bond is issued and paid for, and your investment plan is approved by the Court, the Court issues a document to you to prove that you, as the guardian, have the authority to accept the money from the insurance company on behalf of the children. You send the proof to the insurance company, and they send you the money in your capacity as guardian of these three guardianships."

"Holy moly—that's a lot of paperwork," Kathy said.

"I know," said Rebecca.

Kathy continued, "OK, so there is this flurry of paperwork, and then I get the money. That's not as bad as I was fearing. Then I can use it to get stuff for the kids. I mean, it's for them, so I can use it for piano lessons, sports equipment, birthday trips and stuff, right?"

"Um, there's more," said Rebecca. "When you get the money, it has to be set aside for the kids. It's *their* money. I mean those investments are in your name as guardian for them. And the Court has a continuing interest. You have a parental obligation to raise your children, so you can't look to their money to pay for their own upbringing, unless you are in dire need.

"If you ever want to use the money from a child's account for his or her benefit, you need to get prior Court approval. To do that, you file a petition with the Court. The petition explains what you want the money for, how much the expenditure will be, and why it is in the child's best interest to spend the child's own money for this item. You may need to explain why you aren't buying the item for the child from your personal funds. You can probably do all of this on paper, so you don't have to actually appear before a judge."

"That's outrageous!" exclaimed Kathy. Janine nodded in agreement.

"Then," Rebecca said, "every year you, as guardian, have to file at Court an account describing the earnings in the guardianship, the expenditures made, and stating what assets remain in the guardianship at the end of that year. This account must balance to the penny. And each year, one expenditure item on the account is the legally required payment for renewing the bond. Plus, there is an annual payment to the Court for reviewing the account."

"This gets worse and worse. You say, 'Every year.' Until when? Until I die???"

"No, no—the guardianship ends for each child when he or she reaches the 'age of majority'—18."

"OK. Then . . . ?"

Rebecca continued, ". . . and after the final account is filed with the Court, and approved, the child gets whatever money is left in the guardianship—at age 18, because, at that time, the child is a legal adult. You can imagine what a mess this is when you're talking about, say, $100,000. You have an 18-year-old with $100,000—I call that the 'red Porsche' provision of the law.

"But in your case, Kathy, you will be handling a pretty modest sum, and you probably won't mind giving it over to your child. You could even set up some money-management lessons with your kids for a couple of years before the money is in their hands."

"So, you're saying that, for this $30,000, I have to file three Court accountings every year and maintain three bonds from some bonding company? Until each child reaches age 18? Is that what you're saying?" Kathy was sounding a little hysterical.

"Uh, yes. That's what the law provides."

"Well, Criminy and Nerts!" Kathy exclaimed. "All these Court filings?!! This is infuriating. I know what's in the best interests of my children, and Ian knew that I knew, and I can't believe that he'd make me go through this. Not to mention the Court costs and—excuse me, Rebecca—lawyer fees."

Kathy cooled down a bit. "It doesn't sound like it's worth it to try to spend their money. We'll be all right without invading it. And really, the kids will be grateful when they reach age 18. I like your idea of giving them money-management lessons when they get a little older so they can be responsible with this inheritance. Although, right now, I can imagine Patty just spending it all on frilly clothes. Already at age five, she's a clothes horse.

"Still, this is annoying," she concluded.

Rebecca spoke again. "I'm with you. This is one of my pet peeves. I don't often run across insurance left directly to a minor while the spouse is still living, but I often see a scenario in which the insurance agent sells a policy to a young husband, who names the wife as the first beneficiary. The agent asks, 'And who will be the contingent beneficiary if your wife does not survive you?' The husband automatically names the children, who might be babes in arms, and the insurance agent says nothing about what would happen if the man and his wife died in the same car accident while the kids are minors. Some of these guys just don't seem to think ahead."

FRANK MERTON TAKES BOBBY TO THE BANK

"Hello, Mr. Merton. Good to see you," said Raul Cabrera, the bank manager at Friendly Bank Branch.

"Hi, Raul. I'd like to introduce my son, Bobby. Bobby, shake hands with Mr. Raul."

"Hello, Mr. Raul. Nice to meetcha," said Bobby as they shook hands.

"A pleasure to meet you, too. What can I do for you today?"

"Well, we're here to celebrate Bobby's 11th birthday today. I told him we could set up a bank account for him for his birthday."

"Congratulations, Bobby! Happy Birthday. Certainly—I'd be happy to help you with that. May I assume you are looking at a savings account?" asked Raul.

Frank confirmed that, adding, "Bobby wants to see his money grow as he adds to his account. We're already talking about what kind of a present he'll get himself later from his savings."

Raul and Bobby talked briefly about the kinds of things Bobby might want to buy for himself; he and his dad had already agreed that he wouldn't buy anything until his account has at least $150 in it. Frank was starting the account with $50.

"Mr. Merton, do you understand that Bobby can't be the only owner of this account?"

"No, I didn't know that. Why not?"

"Because Bobby does not have legal capacity—in legal terms, he has not reached the age of majority. We need to make you or Mrs. Merton a co-owner of the account, so we always have an adult involved in making decisions about the account or removing money from the account. Bobby, you won't be able to take money out by yourself until you are 18 years old."

"That's OK, Mr. Raul. I don't know what this is all about, anyway."

"But," Raul continued, "you can add money to your account whenever you want. And your mom and dad can add to it, too. Do you have any questions?"

"Umm, I don't know. Do I get some kind of paper or something that shows that I have this account?" asked Bobby.

"Yes. We'll give you something today that shows the account is in your name with your dad. And your dad can help you set up a way to check your balance from home on your computer whenever you want."

"Neat! I don't think any of my friends have a bank account," said Bobby.

"And," Raul continued, "every three months, we will send you a report in the mail showing how much money is in your account! Congratulations! I think you can be proud of yourself."

"OK, cool! Thanks, Mr. Raul, and thanks, Dad."

WHO IS IN CHARGE OF A MINOR'S ASSETS?

At the Fourth of July family barbecue, Rusty Dalton stopped his sister Rebecca. "Tell me about this 'transfers to minors' thing. Dad is talking about giving some money to Danny."

"Sure! Wait a second—I need some more mustard. OK, this 'transfers to minors thing,' as you put it, is a way for a kid to have an asset in his own name, with an adult having operational control. Let's say Dad wants to give Danny $5,000. Instead of just putting it into Danny's name, he gives it to you as custodian under the UTMA—that's the Uniform Transfers to Minors Act. Wait—I need more relish on this dog, too.

"Anyway, so, Dad sets up a money market account with $5,000, and the name on the account is 'Russell Dalton, custodian for Danny Dalton under the UTMA.' That makes you a fiduciary, of course, and you are liable to Danny for how you manage the money. The social security number for the money market earnings is Danny's SSN."

"'The Uniform Transfers to Minors Act'? Do I need to know more about this? What's 'uniform'?"

"Well, there's an outfit called the Uniform Law Commission that designs laws and then tries to get the legislature of every state in the union, plus the District of Columbia, to adopt them. By 'designs laws,' I mean they write actual language that a state legislature could adopt to add to the state's own statutes. The idea is to promote uniformity of treatment in all kinds of legal arenas.

"Sometimes the Uniform Law Commissioners are tremendously successful in this effort, such as with the UTMA. But even then, states adopt local variations on the law. With the UTMA, states vary on how long you can delay giving the kid the assets. The age of majority is age 18 in most states, but, in a lot of states, you can extend the UTMA account until the child reaches age 21. In some places, you can go to age 25. In some places, it's different ages, depending on how the child got the money—one age for inheritance, a different one for gifts. So, the states are not completely 'uniform.' But on the whole, given how mobile Americans can be, the Uniform Laws do help you understand what the law might provide even if you move to another state."

"OK—too much information. Let's say Dad sets up this account. I assume that Beth and I can add to it?"

"You can, but I advise against it. That mucks up your own planning. If you keep control over money you are supposedly giving away, there's an issue of whether you have actually given it away! In a bad situation, it might even be considered as part of your estate if you died before Danny had received the money."

"Bec, you just lost me there," complained Rusty.

"Well, the bottom line is that, to keep your own estate situation clean, you should not continue to control any money you give to Danny. You can be the custodian for money from Dad, but you should make someone else custodian for money from you. You could have me be a custodian for money you give to Danny, for example. Then it's out of your hands.

"But you know, Rusty, there are other options, and if you're talking about a lot of money, you probably want to do something different. There are two other options in particular."

Just then a soccer ball bumped Rusty's leg. "OK," he yelled, "I'm on my way." Then, to Rebecca, he said, "I'll call you tomorrow. I think I need to know more about all of this."

The next day, Rusty was on the phone asking, "Rebecca, you said there are better options than the UTMA for giving big amounts of money to Danny. I have heard of Section 529 plans, but I don't know much about them. Is that one of the options you were talking about?"

"Yep," said Rebecca. "And the other one is 2503(c) Trusts."

"You lawyers and your Code sections. OK, so tell me about these things."

"Let's start with Section 529 plans. They are college savings plans. They're kind of neat, because you can put in up to five times the annual gift tax exclusion—that would be $75,000—"

"As if!" exclaimed Rusty.

"OK, but *in theory*, you could give a big chunk of money to a 529 plan administrator to hold and grow for Danny for his college. Every state and many large families of mutual funds sponsor one or more of these plans. Not that you want to take the first one you find; sometimes the commissions are more than you would expect, and those benefit the advisers, not the student-to-be. So—a lawyerly recommendation—you want to read the fine print.

"The idea behind the 529 plan is to invest your contributions in a way that's conservative but designed for growth. The plan documents will describe how the administrator plans to invest. Obviously, the longer the assets are in the plan, the more time they have to grow. There's no current income tax on the assets, even when they are sold, and the proceeds are reinvested within the plan."

"Whereas if I sold and reinvested these investments myself, I'd be paying capital gains tax," said Rusty.

"Right. So, if you were to give the maximum amount—I know, you don't have a spare $75,000—but if you did, you would not be able to make any annual exclusion gifts to Danny for five years, because the idea is that you made five years worth of gifts up front."

"And I guess Beth could also give to a 529 plan? I mean, both parents can do this—right?" asked Rusty.

"Oh, sure! I didn't mean to exclude her. The amounts would double. Anyway, when Danny's ready to go to college, the funds are there to help pay for it. Or even pay for the whole thing, depending on the cost of his schooling and how the 529 plan has grown."

"All right. Just getting the outline here. What is the other thing you mentioned? The other Tax Code number?"

"Internal Revenue Code Section 2503(c) Trusts. With a 2503(c) Trust, you need to have a document written up by a lawyer. It's not just a matter of signing some forms that a mutual fund company or the government gives you and then handing over a check," said Rebecca.

"OK, stop right there. I think I'll just go with the 529 plan for now. At this point in our lives, we want to focus on saving for our own retirement and Danny's education, and if I don't need to involve a lawyer, all the better. No offense!" said Rusty.

"Fair enough! See you at Mom's next week?"

GIVING THE KIDS A CUSHION

"John," Claire asked her husband, "have you ever thought about setting the children up with some money now? I mean, we will have their college years covered with the 529 plans, but we have more money than we use, and I think it would be nice to give them a cushion until they get their first jobs."

"Hah! Can you imagine those kids working serious jobs, Claire!?"

"Well, it *could* happen," she chuckled. Mimi and Creighton were in single-digit ages, so it was a stretch to imagine them as adults. Their current career ambitions were "Movie Star" and "Astronaut."

John asked, "What made you think of this now, Claire?"

"So, you know my friend, Rebecca Dalton, the trusts and estates lawyer. Well, I saw her at the gym today. We happened to finish working out at the same time, so we went for coffee, and we got on the subject of the children. She was impressed that we had the kids' college years covered—I told her a lot of it was from your dad. And then we started to talk about how hard it is for young folks to get that first job. You know, you need experience to get a job, but you can't get experience unless you have a job."

"Boy, do I remember those days!"

"Anyway, Rebecca asked if we had thought about giving them a cushion. I told her I expected we would just be there to help as needed, but she scotched that idea."

John looked puzzled. "What's the matter with that?"

"Well, she pointed out that it's possible that we wouldn't be around or that we wouldn't be *compos mentis*, when the time comes. Even if that is unlikely, she also mentioned that there is a limit on the amount of gifts we can give the kids without being legally required to file a gift tax return."

"What the flaming H is a 'gift tax return'? Don't we pay enough tax anyway?"

"Hang on!" Claire chuckled at John's little outburst. "As I understand it, this is a return filed by someone making a gift that's not exempt for gift tax purposes. There's not necessarily a tax to be paid with it—it's informational, for the I.R.S. We don't think about it, because we don't tend to give anyone more than $15,000 combined gifts in a year—much less $30,000 for the two of us—and you don't have to file a return below that. For us, there would be no tax due with the return—it just informs the I.R.S. about how much of the lifetime gift allowance we have used up, and that's so big that it's irrelevant for us.

"Should we set up a meeting with Rebecca to find out more?" suggested Claire. "We have now reached the end of my knowledge on the subject."

A week later, the three of them met. John and Claire had recounted the discussion that brought them there, so Rebecca picked up at that point.

"Well, if you want to build up some funds in your children's names, there are two main relatively easy options: a Uniform Transfers to Minors Account . . ."

"Which the kid gets at age 21," interjected John.

"Yes . . . and a Section 2503(c) Trust, named for the section of the Internal Revenue Code that sets the parameters. With a 2503(c) Trust, you have more formality but also more flexibility.

"Before I describe it more, do you know which gifts you can make that are not 'taxable'? By 'taxable,' I mean gifts for which a gift tax return is due, not that there is necessarily a tax. But, do you know what kinds of gifts you can make that do not require you to file a gift tax return?"

"Umm, no," they both replied.

"Well, gifts between U.S.-citizen spouses are not taxable. Nor are expenses of raising a child, because raising a child is an obligation of a parent, and that means that paying these expenses is not making a gift but paying an obligation. Interestingly, the cost of sending a child to college after he has reached the age of majority—and is thus a legal adult—has not always clearly been understood to be a parental obligation, but the question is not much discussed now.

"Other gifts that do not require filing a gift tax return are payment of medical expenses for anyone, related to you or not, as long as these payments are made directly to the provider of the service—that is, not through the patient or other human responsible for the patient. Similarly, educational expenses, such as tuition, paid directly to a school for the benefit of a student, do not require filing a gift tax return.

"Finally, accumulated gifts of up to a certain amount each year—this year, it's $15,000, but the annual amount goes up now and then—do not trigger filing a gift tax return, as long as the gift is 'of a present interest,' which is to say, it's immediately available to the donee."

"The 'donee' being the person who got money from the 'donor'?" asked Claire.

"Yes! Sorry, I slip into legalese sometimes," Rebecca apologized.

"Whew! That's a lot of information. Let me recap," said John. "Gifts for which we don't have to file a gift tax return include gifts between the two of us, sending the kids to college, paying their tuition for graduate school, paying their medical bills, buying them birthday presents and other gifts, up to a value of $15,000 per year, per parent."

"Right. And you will note that, in all of these cases, the donee has immediate benefit of the gift. What you don't see in that list is an arrangement in which a pot of money is put away for a child for use in the future," pointed out Rebecca.

"Remember how I said the $15,000 gifts were free of the gift tax return filing requirement IF they were immediately available? Well, you don't really want to make $15,000 immediately available to an eight year-old. Congress figured this out.

"Recognizing the position this put parents in who wanted to help their kids build up a nest egg, Congress added Section 2503(c) to the Internal Revenue Code declaring that, under the particular circumstances of a Trust meeting the requirements of that Code section, a gift to the Trust would be deemed to be a gift of a 'present interest.' It's *not*, really, because the Trustee controls it, but this little fiction allows parents to do what they want—give the child money in a deferred way without triggering a gift tax filing requirement," said Rebecca.

"What does the Trustee do with it?" John asked.

"What any Trustee does—invests it carefully. The idea is to build up the Trust. The Trustee pays taxes, keeps the assets safe. When the child reaches age 21, the child gets the money, except that just about all of these Trusts have a neat little device that is allowed by the Internal Revenue Code."

"Well, if we have to give it to the children at age 21, this 2503(c) Trust seems no better than a 'transfers to minors' account. And it would be a lot more expensive to set up," noted John.

"Right you are. But the neat little device I just mentioned allows you to extend the time. It works this way: the Trust document will call for a time-period window, usually 30 or 60 days, that starts when the child turns 21. When the window is open, the child can take out the Trust assets—part or all of them. If he does not take out the assets during this time, the window closes, and the Trust continues until the child is somewhat older, like 30."

"Oh, that's cool," said John. "So, I could set up a Trust for Mimi and give the Trustee $15,000 every year without filing a gift tax return. When she's 21, she has a month to take the money out. I assume we have to tell her she has this right. And if she doesn't take it, the funds stay in Trust until she's 30, 35, or whatever age I have picked?"

"Exactly. Yes, you do have to tell her she has the right to the money. But you still have some leverage: I know that some parents tell their child that, if they take out the money, the spigot is turned off. No more $15,000 annual gifts."

"Can we use this money for their college, if it turns out the 529 plans fall short?" asked Claire.

"You can, although some would see that as distributing the money to you and not for the benefit of your child, because such payments relieve you of paying a parental support obligation. But if you did that, you could be wasting your annual exclusion gifts to make payments that would already be exempt from gift tax. If you add the maximum exclusion gifts every year to the 2503(c) Trust, you can still pay tuition and other college expenses, too, without incurring a gift tax obligation."

"OK. This sounds like a neat idea," exclaimed Claire. "Thanks."

CHAPTER
NINE

CHARITY

What considerations go into making a charitable gift in a Will? Are there other ways to benefit charity that one should consider in setting up an estate plan?

ROGER ASKS BEN A SERIOUS QUESTION ABOUT CHARITABLE BEQUESTS

"Hey, Ben," Roger puffed after their afternoon walk. "Louise and I went to a charity event last night for an outfit that looks out for battered women. It sounds like a really worthy cause, and I'd like to do something for them—along with a bunch of other charities I like."

"That's great, Roger. Are you talking about now or after you're gone?"

"Some of each, I think. But I don't know if I can decide amounts," said Roger.

"How can I help?"

"Well, what are my options?"

"As to the part you want to give after you're gone, the simplest option is to just provide a gift in your Will of X amount to the charity of your choice. But it sounds like you're uncertain, so there is another possibility, which is to leave it up to your PR to decide. But you have to do it the right way!" cautioned Ben.

"What's 'the right way'?"

"Well, first you have the issue of identifying the charity, so that no mistake can be made after you die. So, if the charity has a national office and a state office, you want to identify the one you intend to benefit. Usually you just put the address right in the Will, along with the official name of the charity. It's not always the name by which you know it.

"If you have a bunch of charities you like and aren't sure how to divide up your help among them, you can give your PR some latitude, within limits. I say, 'within limits' because, in order for your estate to get any benefit from making a charitable bequest, it has to be '*from*' you."

"Well, it's going to be *my* money, so it's '*from*' me—no?" asked Roger.

"You would think. But there was a memorable case a long time ago in which a doctor's Will gave his PR discretion to make charitable gifts. It then named non-charitable beneficiaries to get whatever amount did not go to charity. The Will did not direct the PR to give any particular percentage or assets out of the estate to charity—it just left the decision up to the PR. So, the PR gave away 99 percent of the estate to various charities. Lo and behold, there was a huge tax burden, because the charitable deduction was denied. The Will did not specify that 99 percent was to go to charity—those charitable gifts didn't come 'from' the doctor, but 'from' the PR's exercise of his discretion!"

"You've got to be kidding!" said Roger.

"No, it's true! There's an easy way around this: you could give your PR discretion but specify the percentage of your estate that the PR *must* give to charity and specify that any charity the PR names must be one that would qualify for a charitable deduction. That would work fine, because it's clear that you are the one requiring the charitable contribution.

"You could name a bunch of charities, or maybe just say the PR shall give X percent to qualified charities you had donated to within the last three years of your life, or give some other kind of guidance," said Ben.

"I'm going to tell you something else that a lot of people never give a moment's thought to: the charity does not have to accept your donation."

Roger exclaimed, "What!?!?!"

"Right. The kind of gift a charity loves is money. Cash on the barrelhead, with no strings attached. But, of course, a rich donor giving a lot of money to his college might add a few strings. He might want them to name a building after him, establish a scholarship fund for electrical engineering students from Newark, New Jersey, etc.—you know. A more modestly endowed donor might want the contribution to be used only for radio public service announcements, or something."

"And the school would have to do that?" asked Roger.

"Maybe not. There could be a lot of negotiation between the donor and the charity about what limitations the charity will agree to. And after they take the money, the charity might find circumstances have changed and they can't continue to comply with the agreement. Maybe a requirement to invest in only a certain way no longer makes sense, for example.

"But when I talk about the charity not necessarily accepting a gift, I'm thinking not so much about money as about stuff people want to get rid of. Artwork, furniture they think might be 'museum quality.' A museum doesn't have to take it, and then the PR has to deal with an alternative disposition.

"My point is: if you want to give anything other than an unrestricted gift of money to a charity, you might want to make sure in advance that the charity is willing to take it. Could save a lot of time and effort after you're gone," said Ben.

PAIGE CALLS WITH A QUESTION

"Hi, Rebecca. Do you have a couple of minutes to talk about the documents you sent me before I come in to sign them?" asked Paige Ridley.

"Sure! What's up?"

"Well, one main thing: I see that you left out of my draft Will my $75,000 bequest to my college, Rah Rah University. What happened?"

"Oh, yes. I meant to mention that in the cover letter. After I reviewed the financial papers you brought me, I saw that you had a much better option for your gift to Rah Rah than including it in your Will. I recommend that you give Rah Rah $75,000 from your IRA instead of from your Probate estate. That's why I drafted it into your IRA beneficiary designation."

"Oh, I guess I haven't read that yet. But what difference does it make if it's in the Will or the beneficiary designation?" asked Paige.

"Tax savings. Your sister Kelsey is your residuary beneficiary, and the only other big beneficiary of your estate plan is Rah Rah. By giving the charitable donation from the IRA instead of under your Will, you will save your sister probably $25,000 of income tax."

"What!!?? Well, that's cool, but could you please explain it to me?"

"Sure. Here's how it works: as you know, Paige, the money in your IRA was earned by you, but no income tax was charged to you on the money contributed to the IRA, because it is a tax-favored type of account. Over the years, Major Custodian, Inc., who holds your IRA, has invested the IRA money in stocks and mutual funds, and these investments have earned their own income. Major Custodian had to report these earnings to the I.R.S., but you never had to pay tax on that income, either. So, it's essentially tax-free income on a pot of income that was itself tax-free.

"This is a terrific deal, and IRAs are very popular. But this freedom from tax is just a deferral, not a forgiveness of taxes. The tax bill is presented and due when you, or your IRA beneficiary, receives a payout from the IRA."

"OK, I get it. As long as the money is in my IRA, nobody is paying tax on it, and when I take it out, it's treated like income to me. But if it goes to my sister, it's also treated like income to her?"

"Yes—she pays tax, too, if and when it goes out to her."

"Well, I don't want to leave it to someone else just to keep her from having to pay tax! Do I?" asked Paige. "Where are we going with this?"

"OK, your IRA is larger than $75,000. Let's say you leave your entire IRA to Kelsey. You die. Boom, the tax bill has to be paid by her when she gets the money. She pays income tax at whatever her tax rate is—both to the I.R.S. and to her state.

"Now let's say that we take Rah Rah out of your Will. That means there is $75,000 more to go to Kelsey under your Will. Then we give Rah Rah $75,000 from the IRA. As you know, Rah Rah does not pay tax! So, if you give the IRA, or part of it, to Rah Rah, they get the full amount you have left them, without any tax obligation.

"If you do this, the $75,000 that did not have to come out of your Probate estate to pay Rah Rah's bequest is left in there for Kelsey, your 'residuary beneficiary.' She pays no income tax on what she gets under your Will.

"In other words, by doing it this way, you will have converted the $75,000 taxable bequest to Kelsey to a $75,000 tax-free bequest. That could save her $25,000 of income taxes, or even more, depending on her bracket," concluded Rebecca.

"OK. Let me say this back to you to be sure I have it," said Paige. "Instead of leaving Rah Rah $75,000 under my Will, I leave it to them in the IRA beneficiary designation. That leaves $75,000 more to go to Kelsey under my Will because she is my 'residuary beneficiary,' and she gets whatever is left in my Probate estate after my debts and administration expenses are paid. Kelsey does not pay tax on what she gets under the Will. There is $75,000 less to go to Kelsey under the IRA, then, but that's OK, because she's getting that much more under the Will. And Kelsey will be happy because I am saving her a bunch of income tax by doing it this way. Did I get that right?"

"You sure did!" says Rebecca. "The party left in the cold here is the government, who, after all these years of waiting, never does get to collect taxes on $75,000 of that IRA. But we are not legally obligated to arrange our affairs to pay the maximum amount of tax possible."

"Oh, cool!" said Paige. "So, by extension, if I left my IRA to Person A and an equal amount of my Probate estate to Person B, I would really not be treating them equally. Person A's inheritance would be reduced by maybe 35 to 40 percent for the federal, state, and local income tax she'd have to pay, but Person B would get the whole amount free of tax. I never thought about the taxes!"

"Right, you got it! Did you have another question?"

"Nope, that's all. I'll read the rest of my documents now! Thanks!"

PART THREE

Ancillary
Documents

CHAPTER
TEN

FINANCIAL POWERS
OF ATTORNEY

Does everyone need a power of attorney? What is an "attorney in fact"? What can the attorney in fact do with your money? If you have a Revocable Trust, do you still need a POA?

A QUESTION OF ATTORNEY

"Hey, Teddy," Jake remembered, as they were toweling off after a few games of Horse, "I wanted to ask you something. Would you agree to be my attorney?"

"Jake! You know I'm not a lawyer!"

"No, no. I mean on my Power of Attorney. Attorney in fact, not attorney at law. Like an agent."

"Oh, OK. What's involved in it?" asked Teddy.

"Well, it means that you would take over my finances if I became incapacitated."

"Jake, you're only 35. What's going on? Are you sick, or something?"

"Oh, no—just responsible," said Jake. "I guess my friend Mark's accident made me think about it. He got hit by a bus, and it was touch-and-go for a while. It made me think that old thing about 'getting hit by a bus' *is* a 'thing,' because it actually happens. He was on his bike, and he zigged when he should have zagged. He's going to be fine in the long run, but he could have been left alive but unable to function, and that would have been a mess."

Teddy said, "Well, don't you be running in front of any buses! Can you tell me a little more about what I would be agreeing to do?"

"Sure! Let's go for a brew, and I can outline it for you. I'm really grateful that you would consider doing this."

Half an hour later, Jake and Teddy were settled in Scoop's at a quiet table in back, and Jake told Teddy about his recent talk with Rebecca Dalton. "So, this lawyer said I have a much better chance of becoming incapacitated before age 65 than I do of dying before age 65. I had never thought about that! And if I were incapacitated, someone would have to manage my finances—such as they are. And I would rather choose who that is than leave it up to the vagaries of legal procedures."

"What does 'manage' mean, Jake?"

"Well, it means that my agent—my attorney in fact—would assume responsibility for my account at Friendly Regional Bank, my account at Nationally Advertised Brokerage, my condo, my car—in short, every financially meaningful asset I own. That person would be my fiduciary."

"Big word—'fiduciary'! You mean the person would be responsible to manage your assets the way you would if you could?" asked Teddy.

"Close, but really, it's narrower than that. The fiduciary would have responsibility to manage my assets only for *my* benefit. That is, unless I gave the person broader authority—and in writing—to use my assets for other people, that person could not necessarily do everything I might do with my own money. Like buy my son a car. Spend $10 a week on lottery tickets. Invest in a starving upcoming artist. You know, none of that. Stay boring—that's the key.

"So as my agent/fiduciary, you'd make sure my bills were paid, that my money was being managed to keep me comfortable for my expected lifetime, that I had safe investments, food, medical care, clothing and shelter, and a reasonable amount of entertainment, in other words. And if I ever regained capacity to manage my money myself, you'd be off the hook."

"Sounds doable. I've seen how hard you go on the basketball court. Are you sure you're going to stay in shape?" asked Teddy.

"Well, it wouldn't matter if I wrecked my back—I mean from your standpoint. I'd need you to take over only if I didn't have the *mental* ability to manage my affairs. My body could be weak and broken, but if I retained my current exquisite mental sharpness, I could keep up my own finances."

Teddy agreed to take on the responsibility. Jake asked him to go to the lawyer's office to countersign the Power of Attorney document. The document provided that, in event of Jake's incapacity, Teddy was to take over.

Teddy had a question for the lawyer. "Rebecca, if something happens to Jake, how do I prove that Jake is incapacitated and that it's time for me to take charge?"

"OK. Well, since your power 'springs' into effect only if Jake becomes incapacitated, the way you would prove that Jake is incapacitated is set out here in the document. You see here in the third paragraph, where it says the proof is a letter from Jake's attending physician stating that he is unable to manage his financial affairs? Sometimes the client wants the Power of Attorney document to require two letters, but Jake was comfortable with one.

"In fact," continued Rebecca, "I have done a number of Powers of Attorney in which the principal—that's Jake, in this case—says that, even without a letter from a doctor, the agent can simply swear in writing that the principal is incapacitated, and anyone else can rely on that as the trigger. But most clients want to require a doctor's letter."

"Why do I need to sign this?" asked Teddy.

"It's just a precaution. First, it shows that you were aware that you had agreed to assume this responsibility, but, more important, it makes it harder for another person to imperson-ate you and take over Jake's finances. They'd have to mimic your signature.

"And, since this is all about convincing the gatekeepers that you, Teddy, are to step into Jake's shoes, we often recom-mend that you go to Friendly Regional Bank and Nationally Advertised Brokerage and fill out their Power of Attorney forms, too. They don't have legal authority to deny the validity of this form you have just signed, but many institutions are stuck on their own forms, and there can be a delay in getting them to accept a perfectly legal form that is not their own. I have written this one to coordinate with those. It's quite annoying, but generally, I just suggest caving in and saving the fight for other times."

"That's weird," said Jake, "and I suppose we can't put the 'springing' language into the bank forms, either."

"You're right. If you aren't comfortable about this gap between what you have thought out and what the banks provide, you can skip their forms," said Rebecca.

"The other thing I recommend is that clients update their Powers of Attorney pretty often—every three to five years. That reduces resistance in some of these institutions—not that I'm talking about Jake's in particular," said Rebecca.

DWAYNE AND CYRUS DISCUSS POAs

"Hey, Dwayne," called Cyrus, as he exited Rebecca Dalton's office and ran into his buddy.

"How's it going, Cy?"

"Great. Just getting my stuff in order, signing my POA. I had to update it, 'cause it was three years old, and I don't want anyone wondering if I still wanted it the way I had it."

"Ah," said Dwayne. "Well, I don't need one of those. I have a Revocable Trust."

"What do you mean, you don't need it? Is everything you own in your Revocable Trust?"

"I think so. Like what?" asked Dwayne.

"What about your truck? Is it registered in the name of your Trust?"

"Well, no. It's in my name."

"And don't you have an IRA?" asked Cyrus.

"Yeeessss," said Dwayne.

"So, that's not in your Trust, because it can't be. And what about things like refunds, if you paid in advance for something and needed to cancel it? And I bet, if you think about it, there are some other things you own in your own name that might need to be managed.

"If something had to be done with those things, and you weren't able to act, the attorney in fact on your POA could handle the matter—if you had one. Excuse me, but I did just come from my lawyer's office.

"Have you thought about all the things that person might do—like adding assets to your Revocable Trust, buying insurance for you, choosing payouts from retirement plans, continuing a pattern of charitable giving, settling lawsuits, entering your safe deposit box? Guess I'm getting a little preachy here."

"Hmm," said Dwayne. "Well, you've given me a few 'ifs' I hadn't thought about."

Cyrus continued, "And, now that you have me going, what about your house?"

"Heck, Della and I own the house jointly! It's not in my Revocable Trust."

Cyrus responded, "And if she died, it would be another asset in your individual name, along with any other jointly owned assets you two had. And if nobody had your POA—and if you'd lost your smarts—all of that stuff would go through Probate at your death. At least, with a POA, you can name an agent to move all of that stuff into your Revocable Trust, to be managed along with everything else."

"OK, OK, Cy. I think you just added an item to my To Do List. Thanks. Gotta go!"

Expanding on the topic, Cyrus asked, "Before you go, did you know that, in a POA, you can require your agent to make a regular report to a third party, so there's always someone to check on what the agent is doing? Or that you can require a second signature for large transactions?"

"Well, like I said, most of my stuff is in the Revocable Trust, but I will talk to a lawyer about all of this. I guess it's good I ran into you," said Dwayne. "'Bye, for now!"

"It's not so bad, really," said Cyrus. "There's even a Power of Attorney form you can use right in our state law."

"OK. Well, that's good to know. Thanks again, Cy. I really have to get going now."

BEN AND ROGER HAVE A BEER

"Hi, Rog. I'm so glad you suggested a leisurely walk to the park today instead of our ordinary marathon. Let's finish off by dropping in at Scoop's."

"Right you are, Ben. And I want you to know I have been thinking about estate planning some more."

"Oh, really?" The two settled into a booth and gave their order. "Plus lots of pretzels, please," Ben directed the waiter.

"So, Ben, as you know, Louise and I are finally getting around to thinking about setting up a plan to consider how to approach scheduling a time to update our estate plan."

"Oh, for goodness' sake, Roger—just call Rebecca Dalton, and get on with it."

"I know, Ben, but I did want to ask about Powers of Attorney. Louise found some online that are just part of the law here."

"Well, those can be good, all right, because, in our state, the law provides that, if you use the statutory form, any bank or whatever that refuses to honor it has to pay the expenses of fighting that refusal."

"You mean banks don't always honor Powers of Attorney?"

"No! The sad fact is that they don't. If you use their own forms, you're usually not going to have a problem—and, in fact, I would tell clients to fill out the bank form in addition to the POA form we did in the office, just to avoid this problem. But it's not wholly satisfactory. And, of course, the lawyer has to be sure one document doesn't cancel the other!

"In the estate planning world, one fly in the ointment has always been to get some officials to do their jobs without a lot of argument. One of these recurring problems has been getting a bank to let the agent named in a legitimate Power of Attorney actually take over from the incapacitated principal. Same with transfer agents for stocks."

"Really? Louise and I have a lot of stock certificates."

"Roger!!!!! I can't believe you never mentioned this to me before. Please do not keep your certificates. For one thing, you could lose them. For another, it's a pain to transfer them after you're dead—and even harder if you're alive but incapacitated. Just bite the bullet, and transfer all of your stocks into an account with any brokerage that appeals to you. Then, you have to deal with only one official—the one at that brokerage.

"Do you want me to tell you about all the paperwork that is involved for each stock issue that has to be transferred after you die? It would raise the hair on your head, if you had any. You need like five pieces of paper for each company. And if you have lost a certificate—maybe from a stock split—you have to buy an insurance policy to cover it."

"Yikes. OK. We'll call Rebecca and get an appointment ASAP. I have been worried about that failure to honor Powers of Attorney—I've heard about that from some other friends."

"Yes. But between you and Louise, you could minimize the problem by making the Power effective immediately. It does not have to be a 'springing' Power that becomes effective only in the event of incapacity. It can be immediate."

"That sounds fine for Louise and me."

"But it does have to be 'durable.'"

"What's that?" asked Roger.

"Under ancient law, you could not give someone a power you did not have yourself."

"Like the power to sell the Brooklyn Bridge, since I don't own it?"

"Yes, like that," said Ben, "but also like the power to manage your finances if you lose the ability to do so yourself. It may sound like a technicality, but it isn't! Allowing someone to manage your money when you have lost your ability to do so *is* giving a power greater than you will possess, should you lose that power. It was already the second half of the 20th century when finally every state and the District of Columbia had adopted legislation allowing for a 'durable' power of attorney. It 'endures' after you lose your marbles."

"Of course, I have to actually *have* my marbles when I set it up!"

"Yeah, well—there is that!"

CHAPTER
ELEVEN

DOCUMENTS PERTAINING TO HEALTH CARE DECISIONS

Who needs an Advance Medical Directive? Who can witness such a document? How do I ensure that my wishes are followed if I'm found in an unresponsive state?

BARB CALLS HER MOM

"Mom? It's Barb."

"Yes, I know your voice," Mrs. Alcott said dryly. "How are you?"

"Well, I'm fine, but I've been talking with Alex about our estate planning documents, and I'm wondering if I can put you on my Advance Medical Directive."

"'Advanced Medical Directive'?" asked Mrs. A.

"No, Mom—it's an *advance* directive, meaning it's in advance of when it's needed. Not an 'advanced' document, as in highly evolved. It's for making health care decisions about me if I'm not capable and Alex is not around. I'm putting him in charge first, since he's my husband, and we have talked about what I would want, but I would like you to handle this if he can't, for some reason."

"That sounds fine, but I'd like to know more about it. Can you come over tomorrow and explain it?"

"Sure! I'll be there around 2:30."

The next day Barb showed up with a complicated chart of kinds of treatments she might choose to have or not have, a list of factors that would affect her decision, and a draft of the actual document she was considering signing.

"See, Mom? Here's a list of things they might want to do to me in a hospital. I'd like to talk these over with you. But you can see that the actual form in which I would give you this power is somewhat simpler. Basically, if I'm in debilitating pain that the doctors can't relieve, and if I'm suffering from dementia that doesn't look like it will be reversible, I want only comfort care."

"Wow. This looks like something I should have for myself. When you have done yours, would you just get your lawyer to do one for me? I'll have you and your brother witness it," said Mrs. A.

"Oh, no. You shouldn't just copy what I have. You really need to think about what kinds of care you would want. The options don't all have to be in the form, but you need to communicate them to whomever you would name to have this power."

"That's you and Tom, dear," said Mrs. Alcott.

"OK, thanks. And this is important: Tom and I can't witness it. This can't be witnessed by a health care provider or by anyone who might gain from your death—not to be gruesome. Even if you named another agent, I couldn't witness the document. My lawyer made this very clear to us. It probably means you need to sign in some office somewhere."

"OK. I guess that makes sense," said Mrs. Alcott. "What's this other part here?"

"That's the 'living Will' part of the AMD. The AMD can have two parts—one is the section where you name someone to make medical decisions on your behalf, if you can't do it yourself. That's the part where I'm naming Alex—then you—to make these decisions.

"The other part is where you tell the doctor that, if you are close to death, the doctor can let you die and can give you medications that will ease your pain—even if doing so will hasten your death. That does not allow the doctor to kill you off, but it does give the doctor the OK to consider what will make you comfortable if you are already near death," Barb explained. "Anyway, you want to be sure your doctor knows that you have an AMD, so it's good to give her a copy."

"Hmm. Well, this sounds good. If you will give me your lawyer's name and number, I think I should get one of these AMDs, too."

BARB LEARNS ABOUT POLST

"OK, Rebecca. I talked to Alex and my mother, and they have agreed to make medical decisions for me if I can't do it for myself. Is there anything else I need to think about? How about a DNR order? I've heard that some people like to have those in the house in case they need to be picked up by an ambulance and they don't want any special care."

"Ah, yes" said Rebecca. "The 'Do Not Resuscitate' document. This is of greatest interest to people who are already sick. It's not guaranteed to work. The thing is, medical people would much rather make a mistake by keeping you alive. If they're wrong in that direction, you can still die later. If they're wrong in the other direction, it's too late.

"But," said Rebecca, "if you are already terminally ill and really want to be sure the medical establishment will pay attention to your wishes, there's a way to convert your DNR request to a medical order."

"Huh?"

"If an EMT or other medical person sees proof that a doctor has ordered that you be allowed to die, or that some other particular treatment be applied if you are unresponsive, they don't need to assume responsibility themselves."

"So, who does claim responsibility?" asked Barb.

"The law here allows for a Physician Order for Life Sustaining Treatment, or 'POLST.' A doctor, only after discussion with an already ill patient, memorializes the informed decisions of the patient as a medical order in the format called for in state law. Ideally, it's written not too far in advance of when it might be needed. You can understand that the more remote the possibility that it will be needed, the more hypothetical, and possibly unreflective of your true wishes, it would be.

"The POLST form varies from state to state, and not all states have this in their law. As I say, it can allow for different levels of treatment if you are discovered in an unresponsive condition. The point is, you discuss this with an actual doctor and make an informed decision; then the doctor converts your decision into a medical order.

"Anyway, since you and Alex are currently healthy, I don't think you need to be thinking about a DNR or a POLST," concluded Rebecca.

PART FOUR

Important Miscellany

CHAPTER
TWELVE

FIDUCIARIES AND CAREGIVERS

What considerations should you take into account in choosing a fiduciary or a set of fiduciaries—do they have to get along? What are some issues raised when children provide care? When others provide care?

THE ISSUE WITH MULTIPLE CHILDREN

"So, Fran, the lawyer said that I should definitely not name my kids to be my Personal Representatives or successor Trustees for my Revocable Trust."

"Wow, Cora. Isn't that a little strange? Why in the world not?" asked Fran, as they were enjoying a little dinner after their regular bridge game had broken up.

"Yeah, that was my reaction, too, but it all made sense when I thought about it. I had planned to name all four of them for both positions.

"First, the lawyer asked me how my kids get along. Of course, I said they got along great. I suppose all parents want to believe that. Then she asked me how often they see each other, and I had to think about it. Jack, in San Francisco, is probably the most gregarious, and he will fly anywhere in the country to see Bobby. And to see Merle and Melanie, too. But the two M's live 50 miles from each other in New Jersey and see each other about once a year, when I have them here for the holidays. Bobby, who is currently living in Tennessee, is a little bit of a mystery, too. Even I don't talk to him much. So when I thought about it, I realized they don't really make much of an effort to see each other, so, maybe they aren't that close, after all."

"Slow down, Cora! Tell me, why did your lawyer need to know this? Can't you name anyone you want to be PR and Trustee?" asked Fran.

"Sure, but the four of them would have to work together. There would be a lot of papers that all four of them would have to sign. If even one of them is slow about doing paperwork, that could hold up things that have to be done. And if they disagreed about something, that would delay the process. And, of course, they're spread around the country, so they'd have to deal with mailing or Fed-Exing the paperwork around. So, some filing deadlines might be missed with four people having to do stuff, even when they don't have 'issues' among them. But when I thought about it, I couldn't be sure my children didn't have 'issues,'" Cora commented.

"What do you do, then? Doesn't it have to be a family member?"

"Oh, no—not really. You can ask a friend, or your lawyer, or accountant, or even a bank that has trust powers. And there are even people out there available to be hired as individual trustees—it's not common, but there are some. They used to practice law, maybe, but now they have a business acting as professional fiduciaries. Fiduciaries are people who manage money for other people."

"I know what a 'fiduciary' is, Cora," said Fran. "I think I'm OK even though I have five children. I named Arlene to manage all of my stuff when I'm gone, but the others are cool with it. It would be just Arlene, but she gets along with the others. They don't want to be bothered, and she has promised to be totally transparent about what she does. There was even a family meeting where they confirmed it was OK with them."

"Were you at the meeting? Sometimes kids like to put on a show for the parent, but if the parent is gone, they behave differently," noted Cora.

"Actually, I was *not* at the meeting—the kids themselves decided that they needed to get some stuff on the table. Well, let me tell you how it came about," said Fran.

"I decided some time ago that I wanted my children to tell me what items of my artwork, clothing, china, furniture, my collections—you know I collect 18th-century European coins and also dolls—anyway, I asked them—out of all of this stuff—what did they want? So, I emailed them, all five of them, and told them I'd like to have them work this out before I was gone. Basically, I didn't want them to fight about it all when I die. Also, I wanted to be sure I didn't get rid of anything that I would later find out one of the kids had hoped to inherit.

Fran continued, "They were resistant to the notion at first. Tears about old mom passing on, and so on. But some of them did have definite ideas about what they wanted—one son and one daughter, in particular. So, Arlene suggested they plan a weekend together to discuss it all. It took some arranging, but we made a sibling reunion out of it—it became kind of a party.

"Anyway, I'm so glad they did that. Out of that fun weekend, I got my list of what everyone wants. They worked out their disputes right then and there, and they elected Arlene to be in charge. Jeff is second-in-command. It had not occurred to me that it would be difficult to have all five of them working together, but I think your lawyer is right."

Cora mused, "It sounds like your kids are on the same page. But I'm not sure about mine. So, one of my tasks now is to figure out whom to name. I actually thought of asking you, since you're a little younger than I am, and you're good with numbers. But then I thought of someone else from church, and he's thinking about it—unless you're really interested!"

"Thanks, Cora, but I hope that guy will do it. I would agree to be backup, if you want."

CHUCK CONSULTS ABOUT TRUSTEES

"Hi, Chuck!" said Rebecca, getting on the phone with her client. She had known this call was coming and had received permission from Chuck's former wife to work with Chuck as an individual client. During their marriage, both of them had been clients. Tessa was still deciding whether to continue with Rebecca, which Chuck had indicated would be all right with him.

"Hi, Bec," said Chuck. "I want to bat around the notion of Trustees with you. As you know, I'm divorced now, so I want to rewrite my Revocable Trust. The whole divorce experience made me kind of wary about trusting anyone! I hope I get over that in time, but, for now, I want to consider how to deal with my Trust."

"Sure, Chuck. You're definitely removing Tessa as Trustee, I gather, even though she is the mother of your children, and your children will be benefiting from this Trust."

"Well, yes. Do you think that's a mistake?"

"Not at all, but since the kids are still quite young, I do think whoever the Trustee is should be able to consult with Tessa about their needs, should you not be there to provide support," Rebecca commented.

"OK. Here's what I have been thinking: I have a couple of really close friends. They know Tessa and the kids, and they have no problems dealing with her or with each other, as far as I know. These guys, Ned and Bjorn, live in the area and are both responsible kinds of guys. But they're both single now, and I don't know if they understand what is involved in raising a kid."

"I don't think you need to worry about that. Tessa will tell them! But of course, when you have two Trustees, you do have to think about a tie-breaker in the event of disagreement."

Chuck paused. "Mmm, yes. What about adding a third Trustee?"

"Sure, and then you could also state that two out of three are sufficient to make a decision. You know, they will be making decisions about investments as well as about distributions."

"Well, could I put one of them in charge of investments?"

"Yes," said Rebecca. "There are ways of narrowing down the responsibilities of each Trustee. The more you fine-tune this, the more complicated it gets, though. You might scare Ned and Bjorn enough that they won't agree to do the job."

"Something to think about, all right. What about firing a Trustee? I won't be here to do it. Is there such a thing?"

"Yup. You can appoint someone, a Trust Protector, who would have the authority to remove a Trustee without going to Court. And you can even provide that person the authority to remove with or without cause."

Chuck confirmed: "You mean this Protector would be able just to say, 'Ned, you're out,' with no particular reason?"

"That's what I'm saying. In point of fact, there would likely *be* a reason—any number of things come to mind—but the Protector would not have to prove to anyone that the reason was sufficient to justify removal."

"So, basically, we're back to where we started: I need to be able to trust the Protector!"

"I know. There is no completely satisfactory solution to this sort of problem. But it is possible that you would be able to trust an outside person who, for reasons of his or her own, would not be in a position to take on the full burden of being a Trustee but would be willing to keep an eye out.

"And, not to be self-serving, this outside person, the Trust Protector, could be a lawyer or accountant," commented Rebecca.

MARVIN'S CAREGIVING SOLUTION

Fran and Cora were having lunch and got back onto the topic of fiduciaries. Cora advised Fran that Harry, from her church, had agreed to be her PR and successor Trustee, and that she had named Fran as a backup.

"That sounds great," said Fran. "It seems funny not to appoint the children, but if there's any question about their ability to work together, it's best not to put them in that position."

"Yes, sometimes I think it would have been easier to have just one child! There wouldn't be so many birthdays, anniversaries, spouses, names and birthdays of grandchildren, food preferences, allergies, and surgeries to remember," commented Cora.

"My lawyer, Rebecca, said that, often, widows my age end up relying on one particular child for extra help. Fortunately, Fran, you and I aren't there yet. But when you lean mostly on one child, this can create some resentment. I can understand this!"

"Hah! Cora, I hope I never need to lean on a child," commented Fran. "Although I suppose if I need the help, it's safer for all of us if I don't keep trying to do everything myself. Especially if ladders are involved!"

"What an image!"

"And, of course, the kids WANT to help," said Fran.

"True. Rebecca told me about a true situation involving a brother and sister with a mother who needs help. They both do what they can, but the brother is basically doing all the work of taking care of Mom. So, after a while he begins to feel 'put upon' and underappreciated by sis. And his sister is annoyed because her brother acts like he's completely in charge of their mother. He won't listen to sister's suggestions, as if he thinks she just abdicated any responsibility. And she thinks he feels superior, like he's judging her as being 'inadequately loving.'"

"Wow," commented Fran. "Of course, on some level, the sister is glad her brother is doing so much of the work. And she may feel a little guilt, I suppose, both because he's doing the work and because she's GLAD he's doing the work."

"I know," said Cora. "A lot of feelings roiling around. Rebecca said family mediation can help. It's another one of those situations where advance planning may preserve harmony.

"The problem is that, when the parent dies, the one who has done all the extra work is thinking, or even says out loud, 'Hey, siblings! What about a little meaningful appreciation for me, for all I did?' And the others have to deal with that. My friend Marvin Carhart is thinking about all this now. He's widowed, you know.

"He decided to put this problem before his kids—he has four—while he still had his marbles. He told them that, if any of them ended up doing a lot of work to maintain him, he wanted that child to be paid. If this happens, he told his kids it will be like a real job: FICA withholding, state unemployment insurance tax filing, if it's going to amount to enough of a payment to justify it. Maybe not that level of formality if it's not a huge amount.

"He's working on how to establish a reasonable rate of pay. It would be reviewable once a year and maybe even adjusted automatically every year in accordance with a standard-of-living index. In writing. It's not perfect, but it's a little closer to being equitable than letting one of a bunch of kids take care of everything and then get treated exactly the same in the estate plan as the one in Alaska who barely remembers to call Marvin on his birthday. I don't mean that Marvin actually *has* a kid in Alaska. It's just an example," Cora said.

"And I suppose," noted Fran, "this gets more complicated if the helpful kid is also living with Marvin."

"Oh, yes. Then you have to think of the way *that* will be treated. Is the housing part of the child's compensation? Does that child end up owning the house? The proper balance is probably somewhere along that spectrum," noted Cora. "But the point is to be clear up front. Ideally, all the children end up agreeing. Or, if that can't happen, Marvin—or whoever—explains in writing why Kid X is getting something the others don't have. You can't always get buy-in from a group of people."

"What about the opportunities the caregiving child has to take advantage of the situation?" asked Fran. "I'd want to know if Marvin's kids agreed that the caregiver should report to them and even let them see Marvin's bank statements."

"Hmm," said Cora. "I'll mention that to Marvin the next time I see him."

GLORIA AND SELF-HELP

"Karen, have you talked to Dad lately?" Paul was calling his sister, sounding concerned.

"Well, no, actually. It seems that, every time I call, he's taking a nap, or the doctor is there, or he doesn't feel well enough to come to the phone."

"Yeah, exactly the same things that Gloria is telling me. Bottom line: when is the last time you spoke to him?" asked Paul.

"Mmm, probably a couple of months ago," said Karen.

"And how did he sound then?" Paul was sounding concerned. "I don't like to question Gloria, after we were so lucky to find her. I mean, it took a couple of months for us to find someone to live in, who seemed to be so caring, and who had all that prior experience."

"To tell the truth," Karen responded, "Dad sounded a little distant, and he kept the conversation short. Now I'm getting worried, too."

Paul and Karen were both medical doctors with busy practices, and both lived a couple of hours from their father. But they were their father's only children, and their mother had died. So, when Dad insisted on staying in his home of several decades, despite suffering a bad fall and loss of mobility, they had felt very fortunate to learn of Gloria through Dad's temple. The rabbi knew about Gloria because another congregant, now deceased, had employed her.

Paul and Karen set aside an hour the next day to have a brainstorming session to work on this problem—or possible problem. They sensed that they were going to need at least that much time to deal with their concerns.

Karen called Paul at the appointed hour. "OK, so I had a few ideas. How do you want to proceed?"

"Why don't you tell me your ideas, and I'll react when you're done?"

"OK, here's number one: We got Gloria through the rabbi. Let's call and see if the rabbi has seen Dad lately and get some feedback. I mean, even if Gloria can't take Dad to services, the rabbi should still care about his flock, I think. And I would guess there's some kind of outreach group at the temple that checks on congregants who are at home. We could find out what they think."

Paul said, "That's pretty clever! I hadn't thought about that."

"Second, we could ask Mrs. Goren next door if she has seen Dad, and we could call some of his other neighbors, too."

"I think Mrs. Goren moved to Minnesota to be closer to her children, but I will make a list of the neighbors I can think of, and maybe you can add some more," volunteered Paul. "And friends—didn't he have a regular bridge group? Even if he's not mobile, they could go to his house to play, couldn't they?"

"Good! OK, third on my list: I think I remember the name of Dad's attorney, and we could call him. Harry Stenkel, or something like that. I'm looking for his information."

"Good work, Karen. These are great suggestions. Any more?" asked Paul.

"Yes. I mean, I'm sure you thought of this, too. I think I might just 'drop in' on Dad. But I want to gather information first with these other steps."

Paul added, "We should really call his doctors, too, to see if they have seen him lately and what kind of shape he's in. Is he keeping up with his medications? Has he lost more mobility? And so on."

"Oh, yes—I meant to mention that," commented Karen.

"I'm kind of wondering if there are other people in the house. You know, friends of Gloria that we don't know about," noted Paul.

"Yikes, what a thought! Now you're being deeply suspicious. I suppose the next thing you'll want to check is the deed on the house—whether it's still in Dad's name," said Karen.

"Hah! Who's being deeply suspicious now? But, truthfully, if Dad tried to sign the house over to Gloria—and I assume that's what you were suggesting—wouldn't the lawyer they hired for the deed figure out that something wasn't legit and refuse to handle it?" Paul asked.

"Who knows? Maybe Dad told the attorney that his kids are out of touch—not through any fault of our own—and he wants to do something significant for Gloria. And really, what's to keep him from adding her to his bank and brokerage accounts?"

Karen continued, "Man, I was already worried when you called yesterday, but now I'm terrified! Dad could be really isolated. If all of his buddies are as cut off from him as we have been in the last couple of months, Dad can't be having a great time. It's like being a prisoner."

"Right. No quality of life for him, but perhaps Gloria's standard of living has improved substantially. I hate to be so suspicious, but I think we need to check this out ASAP."

"Me, too," said Karen. "Let's divide up these tasks and reconvene by phone tomorrow. 6:30 pm?"

"Sure," said Paul.

ROGER RAISES A QUESTION

"Hey, Ben," Roger greeted his buddy as they were about to begin their day's walk. "Before we get going—I'm sorry to impose again, but this question about fiduciaries bothers me."

"What question is that, Rog?"

"I mean, thinking about putting all the burden of being my Personal Representative and Trustee on Louise when I die—assuming I go first, I mean—it just doesn't seem fair. But I don't want to have the kids do it with Louise, at least not both of them, because that would make three people, and I wouldn't know how to choose between the kids. I guess I could ask Louise which of them should serve. Or maybe Louise doesn't even want to do it, and she'd want the kids to take charge. Or maybe she'd like her sister to work with her. That might be an option, or even better, her brother-in-law—he's in finance. And maybe the kids wouldn't want to do it, anyway. And, well, there are so many options—do you see my problem?"

"Slow down, Roger! I think I do see your problem—you're using this as another excuse to avoid finalizing your estate planning work!" commented Ben.

"Hmm. OK—there may be some truth there. Any ideas for me?"

"Sure!" exclaimed Ben. "Have you thought about a corporate Trustee? By that, I mean the bank you use has a Trust department, and they have professionals who could work with Louise as co-PR and co-Trustee, or they could just do the job completely without burdening the family.

"Corporate Trustees are a great solution in a lot of situations—they have administered thousands of estates. They deal with families all the time and will keep them informed. They know exactly all the steps in administering an estate—how to make any Court filings, how to get proper valuations of your assets, how to divide up an estate between Trusts, how to make outright distributions, how to deal with creditors, when taxes are due, how to file returns. There are hundreds of details to attend to. And corporate Trustees are bonded and insured against any wrongdoing," Ben pointed out.

"And I already know a lot of the folks at the bank," said Roger, getting excited. "I'm sure the banking folks would introduce Louise and me to some of the Trust department folks, so it wouldn't all be strange when I die."

"That's an excellent idea, Rog. For one thing, you want Louise to be comfortable with the Trust officer, and vice versa. And you could talk about their fee structure when you meet. Naturally, they are paid for this work, but you'll have the comfort of knowing they will do the job efficiently and correctly—you don't always have that comfort with an individual."

"Well, thanks. That makes me feel better. Are you up for a couple of turns around the block?"

BEN AND REBECCA MEET FOR LUNCH

"Thanks for meeting me, Ben. I just wanted to see if you had some ideas about something that has been bothering me," Rebecca explained.

"Well, it's always a pleasure to see you, with or without an agenda! And I love Yung Lee's. I'll just have dim sum and some green tea."

They ordered, and Rebecca got to the point of the lunch. "Here's what's on my mind, Ben: A couple of other estate planning lawyers have just been in touch with me recently with essentially the same question, and I'm not sure I have a real answer. Do you know Miranda Lanier and Tony Saenz?"

"No, I don't know them—haven't been keeping up with the new crew of T&E lawyers. What's the question that you might not be able to answer?" asked Ben.

"Well, both Miranda and Tony have been approached by adult children of parents they think are being abused. In Miranda's case, the abuser—sorry, alleged abuser—is a sibling of the person who contacted her. This gal thinks her brother has had his name added to all of their mother's accounts as a joint owner. When she has been at her mother's house, she has seen things like mail from the bank in envelopes addressed to brother and Mom. She doesn't know what to do!"

"Right," commented Ben. "And the real problem is that Mom might have actually wanted to promote the brother over Miranda's client. You can't always tell what the parent wants—perhaps she's overly vulnerable to suggestion, perhaps she is being fed bad information that makes her favor the brother, and perhaps she just figures, for reasons of her own, that the brother should be given these extras."

Ben mused for a moment. Then he asked, "Do you happen to know who does Mom's estate planning work? And does Miranda's client have copies of the documents?"

Rebecca responded, "The documents Miranda has are at least ten years old—not that that's so unusual. I don't know who wrote them. The distributions are to the two siblings equally, the sister and brother. The brother is named as agent in the financial Power of Attorney, and the sister is the health care agent. The fact that Mom trusted the brother for the financial dealings by naming him in the POA, I suppose, suggests that Mom felt comfortable giving him a lot of financial control. But this client is concerned that he's going beyond doing what he should for their mother and is helping himself.

"Perhaps the client could take her mother for some kind of medical checkup, including a cognitive check. But if Mom has her marbles, she might object to that."

"I think there's a way to get Mom to a doctor without suggesting she's loony," said Ben. "But it sure is tricky, because sometimes a person's lucidity appears and then disappears. Even if she gets a clean bill of health, you can't be sure she's not being unduly influenced. Other than just being vigilant and being sure to have a presence in Mom's life, I don't know what to recommend for your friend Miranda's client. Putting Mom's money outside the control of her children might be helpful, but even that is not necessarily a permanent solution."

"What do you mean, Ben?" asked Rebecca.

"Well, if Mom set up a Revocable Trust and moved all her assets into it and named an independent Trustee—not the children but possibly a Trust company—to manage the assets, that might be helpful. But she has to be *compos mentis* to do that. And, let's say she was, and she did. What would happen later, when she, apparently still mentally 'with it,' removed that Trustee and substituted the brother? If she shows no apparent mental disability, the Trustee is not going to fight the removal. Sometimes the bad guy does actually win—if the brother is a genuine bad guy.

"But, from what you have told me, I don't think the sister and Miranda have done everything they could. Brother might be doing these things, but perhaps he is doing them naively, not understanding that there are better ways to manage Mom's finances than putting them into his name. He may even welcome help, and even if he doesn't, he might become more careful if he's confronted with these suspicions," Ben commented.

"Hmmm. Let me think about that. We might be able to do that gently. Should I order another pot of tea?" asked Rebecca.

"Sure, I could use some more. What kind of problem is your other friend, Tony, having?" Ben asked.

"It's pretty bad. In his case, two of the children want to take their mother's caregiver to Court, because they have proof that the caregiver has stolen from her. Tony was contacting me for advice on how to bring the suit. I'll help him as much as I can, but obviously it would have been better not to let things get this far. Do you have any general advice on prevention of abuse?"

"Whew," Ben exhaled. "That is a tough one. The best protection is to avoid isolation. If the parent stops seeing friends and family, that's a red flag. If the parent sounds drugged, or if the caregiver seems to have too much control, especially if she—or he—is like a barrier between parent and these friends and family, that's a red flag. Changed legal documents, unexplained financial activity, missing assets, unpaid bills—all of these are red flags, too, but the children might not be aware of these.

"Almost any older person wants to age in their home. It's familiar, and they know their way around. But, if they move to some kind of continuing care retirement community, where they can graduate from an apartment to assisted living, and so on, they will have lots of activities and can make new friends. That can be really good. Listen to me, going on!" said Ben.

"Moving to be near children," he continued, "which is a commonly considered solution, makes it modestly easier for the children to keep in touch, but, honestly, the children have their own lives, too, and won't likely make the parent the focus of those lives.

"And, of course, not everyone is married with children. NOT that I'm looking at you, particularly, Rebecca, but we can return to that later," chuckled Ben.

"Sometimes the best solution is to live with a child, but if there are multiple children, it's really important to be clear about how the live-in child is to be compensated for giving up his freedom. It's just not fair for the other children to let one kid handle everything and for them to expect not to have the parent compensate them in some way for this care," Ben finished.

"True that," said Rebecca. "It's one of those tough-to-broach arrangements bridging human relations and fiscal relations. Another one is marital agreements."

"Yup, in both cases, the benefits FAR outweigh the discomfort of setting them up. Thanks for lunch, Rebecca."

"You're welcome. Thanks for taking time out of your hectic retirement schedule," laughed Rebecca.

"Hah! You should be so busy," said Ben.

SPECIAL ASSETS:
Tangible Personal Property, Pets,
Life Insurance, Digital Assets

Certain common assets have special characteristics that deserve special attention. By no means are the following comments exhaustive, but they are meant to be useful and cautionary.

TANGIBLE PERSONAL PROPERTY

Tangible personal property (TPP) often creates difficulties in an estate administration all out of proportion to its financial value. This sentence bears repeating. *Tangible personal property* OFFEN *creates difficulties in an estate administration all out of proportion to its financial value.*

When a testator works out in advance how the TPP is to be distributed and communicates these decisions to family and friends, no one need be surprised. This is a blessing for the family. Children may develop attachments to items they grew up with, even small items with no monetary value. Ideally, any conflicts are dealt with while the parent is living—not after death, when no answers are available.

If the testator has recommendations on how to dispose of particular items, he should leave a memorandum for the PR or possibly put advice into the Will.

Appendix A refers to a website with help for making advance arrangements for TPP.

PETS

Our furry and feathered friends and our scaled friends (I once worked on an estate plan to provide for two snakes) require special attention. Who will care for them when we are unable to do so, and what funds will be available for the caretakers?

This is a reminder to think of them in preparing both a Power of Attorney and a Will or Revocable Trust. Please see Appendix A referencing the ASPCA site pertaining to pet Trusts.

LIFE INSURANCE

Life insurance is very useful in estate planning. It can replace assets lost from taxes or debt, it can replace lost income, and it can provide liquidity for anticipated major expenditures such as college tuition and retirement expenses.

One should keep in mind that life insurance has a value both before and at death. During life, the policy's value is minimal if the insurance is term insurance, but potentially quite high if it is whole life insurance. Thus developed the industry of "life settlements," in which the insured, in order to obtain needed funds during life, sells a life insurance policy he owns on his own life to someone else. That new owner collects on the insurance when the insured dies. The new owner might be someone who would not ordinarily have an insurable interest in the insured. Whether a person has an "insurable interest" is a matter of state law.

But insurance has a much greater value at death—you could say the value explodes. If the beneficiary of the insurance is an estate or a Revocable Trust, the insurance proceeds are available to pay for winding up the decedent's affairs. If the beneficiary is an individual, the insurance proceeds escape the decedent's creditors, even including tax authorities.

And, one of the best aspects of this exploded insurance value is that it carries no income tax burden. That is, the beneficiary owes no income tax on account of receiving the insurance proceeds.

DIGITAL ASSETS

Digital assets include social media accounts and assets stored in digital form, such as photographs, documents, journals, music—all of which may have sentimental, if not monetary, value.

In addition, electronically stored digital assets include assets with monetary value, such as cryptocurrency and domain names. It is estimated that there are more than 1500 types of cryptocurrencies, with a monetary value exceeding $200 billion. Domain names can be a valuable part of a business.

There are two issues with such assets. First: they must be adequately described in a document intended to transfer them at death. A direction to distribute "all my personal property" may, or may not, be interpreted as including a cryptocurrency account or a domain name. Second: the asset owner must be sure the fiduciary will have timely access to the private key for a cryptocurrency account or passwords allowing the fiduciary to get to the account to access the value. The law is developing on how barriers to access can be removed for Personal Representatives and others.

PART FIVE

Pulling It All Together

CHAPTER
FOURTEEN

GETTING THE PICTURE

What can you do if the arrangements you are making—your estate plan—just don't coalesce in your head? Can you find another way to look at the plan so that it makes sense to you?

Yes.

There are two things you will want to understand: which assets are controlled by which documents, and what these documents together accomplish in the distribution of your assets.

MINERVA AND THE ASSET TABLE

Minerva Hawkins and Rebecca Dalton have reviewed Minerva's asset situation, and they have produced the following list of assets as a result of the discussion:

Minerva, a divorced woman, owns

her house	$500,000
(mortgage loan of $350K)	(350,000)
a brokerage account joint with son	300,000
furniture, furnishings, car, jewelry	100,000
(called TPP, for "tangible personal property")	
a bank account POD to her sister Hecuba	50,000
an IRA payable to her university	100,000
whole life insurance payable to her estate, death	
benefit value	100,000
inherited beach house, with sister	
Minerva's tenancy in common interest value	75,000

In order to help Minerva understand what documents will control the disposition of these assets *and* in order to help Rebecca prepare those documents, Rebecca has put the asset information into tabular form.

Minerva's table looks like this:

	Will	POD	Joint With Right of Survivorship	Beneficiary Designation
Residence	$500,000 (350,000)			
TPP	100,000			
Major Bank		50,000		
Monster Broker			300,000	
Beach house	75,000			
IRA				100,000
Insurance				death benefit $100,000 paid to estate
(net)	$325,000	$50,000	$300,000	$200,000

After reviewing the table, Rebecca points out a few aspects of it to clarify matters for Minerva:

1. At first blush, it seems that Minerva's Will disposes of $325,000 worth of assets. However, inasmuch as Minerva has made her estate the beneficiary of the insurance, her Will actually controls $425,000. The estate will need the liquidity from the life insurance, as no other Probate asset is liquid. The PR will use the cash to pay Minerva's final income taxes, credit card debt, ongoing mortgage payments (until sale of the house), insurance and real estate tax expenses, expenses of preparing the house for sale, expenses of disposing of (selling, shipping, perhaps

insuring) her tangible personal property, funeral, and costs of administering her estate.

2. The account at Major Bank is not subject to the Will because it will go directly to Minerva's sister, as called for in the Payable on Death designation.

3. The beach house does *not* go directly to Minerva's sister. Because the sisters inherited it, they own it as tenants in common. That is, each sister owns a separate one-half interest in her own name. Each sister is free to dispose of her half as she wishes, at death, or during life, so Minerva needs to consider this when writing her Will. The person to whom she leaves her half of the beach house will own it with Minerva's sister Hecuba, 50–50. The two owners will need to deal with utility bills, insurance, taxes, repairs, scheduling use of the property, and so on. If one owner wishes to sell, and the other can't afford to buy out the seller, there will be conflict.

4. The IRA does not go through the Will. Even if Minerva's Will said where the IRA should go, that statement would be ineffective. It is the beneficiary designation for the IRA that controls where it goes. In this case, she has left it to her university.

5. Joint ownership, the POD designation, and the IRA beneficiary designation together dispose of $450,000.

The Will, even counting the insurance, controls less than her non-Will documents. Minerva is surprised to hear this.

As you see, a simple table of this sort can clarify which documents control which assets and can raise questions to be considered in developing the estate plan. Naturally, the table will be slightly (but not much) more complicated when there is a Revocable Trust, a spouse, and more assets.

DOREEN FOGS OVER

Doreen Lake and Rebecca Dalton had been meeting for almost two hours when Rebecca said she was pretty sure she understood Doreen's assets, her family situation, and her goals.

"So, Doreen," started Rebecca, "here's what I recommend for you."

Doreen listened intently as Rebecca said, "You want to provide for your mother, should she survive you. I suggest putting assets for her into a Trust. Your brother Phil would be the Trustee, as well as your PR, blah, blah, blah and if he blah blah blah.

"And you want to provide for Phil, so I blah blah blah, and for his kids, blah blah blah yadda yadda, because they are too young blah blah blah, yadda yadda."

This was agony. Doreen's body was in the conference room, but, mentally, she was in the coffee shop downstairs ordering a skinny latte and a scone.

Rebecca was still talking. "Blah blah blah, yadda yadda yadda," when at last she said, "Would you like me to draw a picture of how this would work?"

Bingo! Doreen was back in the room, with her first smile in two hours. "Yes! That would be great!"

And a few minutes later, Rebecca gave Doreen the diagram shown on page 213.

This diagram, however crude, helped Doreen understand how her wishes would be carried out when she died. It also enabled her to discuss options with Rebecca that might not have occurred to her without the diagram. If you think a picture would be useful, ask for one.

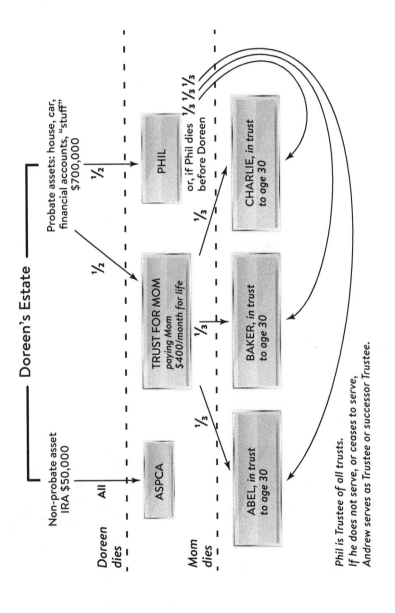

CHAPTER
FIFTEEN

DO I HAVE A PROBLEM?
WHAT SHOULD I DO?

The many sad situations described in the foregoing conversations have all happened, not rarely, but often. If you aren't sure your own estate plan will operate as you wish, here's what you can do:

IS THERE A PROBLEM?

First: *Find your documents*: Find your Will (with all of its Codicils), documents for any Trust you have established or of which you are a beneficiary, your beneficiary designations, and your deeds. Find your Power of Attorney and health care Power of Attorney documents. Do you have the originals, that is, the ink-signed documents? If not, do you know where they are? In the case of the Will, *the original document is the only effective one.* If you do not have it, you need to know who does. It is essential to have the originals or copies of the documents *as they were signed*, and not just preparatory drafts. Changes of only a few words between a draft and the final version could have a big effect on how the document operates.

Second: *Find your asset information and contracts:* Locate your latest bank and brokerage statements, and any contractual arrangements you have in writing that could affect the disposition of your assets: prenuptial or postnuptial marital agreements, promissory notes made *by* you, promissory notes made *to* you, and so on. This step may require some thought. Also, who other than you knows about these contracts? In the case of promissory notes, do you have, or know where to find, a record of payments made?

Third: *Review your documents:* How old are your documents? Do you still want the people you have named in these documents to act as your PR or Trustee? If you have young children, have you named a guardian to raise them if both parents die young? Have you made asset management arrangements (one or more Trusts within these documents) for minor children or other people who will or might need asset management at your death (or if only one other death in addition to yours would need to occur to make that necessary)? Do you know where all the named beneficiaries live? Are all the people named in your documents adequately identified to enable someone else to find them? Do you have any unnecessarily complex distribution arrangements?

Fourth: *Review the titling* on any financial asset you own that has a "title," such as bank and brokerage accounts, real estate, your car, boat, etc. Are you the only named owner on these? Do the "titled" assets all use the same version of your name? If someone else is also named as an owner, can you tell what type of co-ownership you have, for example, joint tenants with right of survivorship or tenancy in common? If you are married to the other owner, do you have a tenancy by the entirety? If you are in a community property state, do you know which assets are your separate property and which are community property? If the document just cites you and another person as "joint tenants," do you know whether, in your state, that creates a right of survivorship? Do you have any POD or TOD accounts? Do you own any asset on which a minor or other financially incapable person is a co-owner?

(*If you live in a community property state or during your marriage have lived in such a state, the name in which the asset is titled may not describe who owns it. A community property asset may be titled in the individual name of a single spouse, and such community property may require special attention.*)

Fifth: *Make a table of your ownership interests.* Set up a table showing five columns with these headings: Will, Revocable Trust, JWROS (two sub-columns: one for assets owned with spouse, and one for assets owned with others, even if the spouse is among them, POD/TOD), and Beneficiary Designations. Under each heading, list the assets that are controlled by the stated documents or form of ownership.

Sixth: *Review your powers of attorney.* How old are they? Are the agents you have named still appropriate? Is their contact information current? Do the powers you have given allow an agent to do everything you would want the agent to be able to do with your money? (Think of care of a pet, charity, regular gifts to friends or family, support contributions to a parent, for example.) Does the agent on your health care Power of Attorney know your allergies, religious and dietary restrictions, and treatment wishes, and is the agent prepared to tell a doctor or hospital what these are?

At this point, you will almost certainly have discovered something you did not know. Here are some common discoveries:

- You have no idea where to find one or more of your important documents.

- You have copies of documents, but you don't know where to find the original, ink-signed documents.

- You have drafts that were never finalized.

- An asset you own with another is not held in the type of ownership you had thought.

- Minor children or others who can't be trusted to manage money will come into possession of funds, or might, if only one other person died and then you died, or the intervening person died soon after you did.

- If you have a Revocable Trust, you find that some of your assets are still in your sole name, instead of in the name "You, as Trustee of the 'Your Name Revocable Trust.'" Those assets will go through Probate.

- You moved out of the state where your documents were done and never had them reviewed for the law of your new state.

- The people you have named as fiduciaries (Personal Representatives, Trustees, persons to care for your minor children in the event both parents die before the children grow up) are dead, incapacitated, out of your life, or totally inappropriate for some other reason.

- Your Powers of Attorney for finances or for health care are more than three years old.

- You married, divorced, had a child, inherited a lot of money, or had some other major life change since the dates on your documents.

If you made one or more such discoveries, you need to take action.

The average person would rather attack a load of ironing, or even have a root canal, than address estate planning issues. But, now that you understand more than you did before you read this book, perhaps you are ready to grapple with your planning.

As the preceding conversations may have made clear, it is cheaper and more efficient to find a qualified lawyer to help you prepare your estate plan than it is do it yourself or with a lawyer not in the estate planning field. I say "help you," because there are numerous decisions *you* need to make during the process. The experienced lawyer will ask the right questions and spell out consequences of one answer over another. Without this kind of legal help, you run a not-insignificant risk of causing heartbreak and large, avoidable legal fees when you are gone.

FIND A LAWYER

1. *How do you find a lawyer?* Many of us don't meet lawyers in our daily lives, much less engage their services. (I had met only two lawyers before I went to law school.)

    If your neighborhood has a website or list service in which the neighbors share helpful hints, you could start there. Make it clear that you want an experienced Trusts and Estates (T&E) lawyer.

    If you know any lawyers at all, you could ask them for recommendations for a specialist in Trusts and Estates law. If you are in a remote location, find an experienced T&E lawyer who will talk to you on the phone, reducing the number of times you will need to meet.

A good resource for locating a T&E lawyer is the American College of Trust and Estate Counsel, or ACTEC, a nationwide organization of lawyers (called "Fellows" of the College) elected by their peers on the basis of mastery of the estate planning legal field and their service to the profession. The College actively works to draft and respond to state and federal legislation, to keep its members educated, and to provide public education on estate planning. There are about 2500 Fellows across the U.S. and some abroad. Look at *www.actec.org.*

Occasionally, a financial adviser works so closely with one attorney that the adviser asks all of his or her clients to use that attorney. If you are happy with the T&E attorney you have, you need not make this change. If the adviser is insistent, make sure the lawyer specializes in T&E.

2.   *Be sure you are comfortable with the lawyer.*

If you are not sure you are comfortable with the first lawyer you interview, talk to another one. This is really important—the T&E lawyer will have to know a lot about you to do the job properly. The lawyer will know about your financial assets and liabilities, your health, your long-term goals, the quality of your marriage, how you feel about your children, your siblings, what values are important to you, and more. You should not feel railroaded or rushed by this person. You need to be comfortable asking this person questions. You need to respect—and have the respect of—this person. The stakes are high.

WHAT WILL THIS COST?

It is true: hiring a lawyer costs money. Also true: people often don't like paying for services. Finally: it's hard for lay persons to be sure they're getting what they need.

Also true: not hiring a qualified lawyer could cause big expenses, injured feelings, and incorrect distributions. You will not know about this, but your loved ones will feel the hurt after you're gone.

You may find yourself receiving advice from insurance agents, financial managers, and others. Yes, this advice will probably be free, and you might think it will save you money. NEVER act on such advice without ensuring that the insurance agent, financial manager, or other adviser knows and can explain how such changes will interact with your estate plan.

Assuming you have found a lawyer, what should you expect?

Some (probably most) lawyers charge for their services on the basis of the amount of time they spend on the work. Some lawyers will quote you a fixed fee to prepare a set of documents. Some will quote you a range. The lawyer should give you a written statement of how the fees are calculated.

Hourly rates can run from, say, $150 or $250 to as much as $1,000 or more for sophisticated tax planning. Hourly rates will vary from one part of the country to another and will reflect the experience of the attorney.

Estate planning work for a new client could take the lawyer ten to twenty hours, or more. The number of hours depends on factors such as how efficiently you use your lawyer (see below), whether previous titling arrangements need to be rearranged, and whether the lawyer needs to negotiate with an IRA or pension trustee or insurance company about beneficiary designation language to fit into your estate plan. Other factors can push the cost up, too, such as planning for family businesses or other complicated assets, the need for tax planning or special needs planning, and more. Further, the lawyer may wish to consult with your accountant, financial planner, or insurance agent about aspects of the plan, with your permission. This will take time.

3. *Use the attorney efficiently.*

   In order to save time with your attorney, be prepared for your meetings:

   a. Respond to any questionnaire the lawyer may send you.

   b. Have in mind your desired disposition of your estate. Who are your beneficiaries, and what proportion of your estate should each one get? Who benefits if the primary beneficiaries do not survive you? Who should be in charge of carrying out your wishes? Who should manage money for those who need help? As you are identifying your beneficiaries, think about special non-family persons in your life, such as a nanny or housekeeper. Think about your pets and charitable programs you support.

c. Take to the initial attorney meeting copies of all existing estate planning documents you can find, with copies of your financial documents, any contracts affecting your financial life, and names and addresses of possible beneficiaries and fiduciaries. If you are copying an original Will, *do not unstaple the pages to make the copy.*

d. Remember the lessons you have learned from this book. What you have learned will save "teaching time" in your meetings with the lawyer.

What will NOT work: bringing in draft documents prepared by others or on a computer program for the lawyer to "tweak." No lawyer I know would agree to "finish up" documents drafted by others. To do that, the lawyer would have to pore over the unfamiliar draft document to be sure it has the numerous technical elements needed in these documents. This would be very time-consuming.

What you are buying from the lawyer is his or her experience and expertise, applied to your unique situation, to accomplish your personal goals. The documents to get the job done are just the final step in this process. Let the lawyer use his or her own document forms.

AFTER THE PLAN IS DONE . . .

4. *Who needs to know, and where should you keep your completed documents?*

    The work you do will have its intended effect only if the necessary documents can be found when they are needed. To optimize the chances of this: a) be sure your fiduciaries know that you have appointed them, and b) tell them where the documents are.

    Where should you put the documents? Consider these options: in your house, with your lawyer, or with the fiduciary himself/herself. Write on any *copies* you retain the location of the *original* documents. If anyone you know might benefit from the disappearance of a document, be particularly thoughtful about how to protect that document and its copies. If you make copies, DO NOT UNSTAPLE your Will.

    Keep in mind this legal presumption: if your Will (the original ink-signed version, not a copy) was last known to be in your hands and it can't be found when you die, the Court may presume that you revoked it. Any prior Will you had made would NOT be revived, because it would have been revoked by that missing Will. You could be found to have died intestate.

5. *How often should you review your plan?*

    You should review your plan every five years to eight years, if nothing startling or unexpected has happened in your life during that time. If you win the lottery, someone important to you dies, the size of your estate goes up or down substantially, you get married or divorced, or have a child or another child, one of your intended beneficiaries develops a drug dependency, etc., then you should look at your documents to see if they still suit your new situation.

6. *How can you ease the burden for your fiduciaries?*

Once you have updated your estate plan thoughtfully and with the appropriate legal help, the best single thing you can do for your family and fiduciaries is to pull together, in one place, all of the information they will need in order to administer your estate. This is a daunting task, but you can complete it bit by bit.

The necessary information will include copies of the documents or a statement of where they can be found, financial information, family information, military-service history, and more. See Appendix B. Make a file or even a three-ring notebook. Date the file or notebook when it is complete, to ensure that you can tell, at a glance, whether it has your latest Power of Attorney, your latest contact information for doctors and others, etc.

CHAPTER
SIXTEEN

FINAL NOTE

In the course of putting this book together, I repeatedly encountered exceptions to what I thought were fairly straightforward propositions. This should not have surprised me, because significant legal differences exist even among the three contiguous states where I practiced. State laws vary, and sometimes widely.

I learned, for example, that in Louisiana, a 16-year-old can make a valid Will. In three states—Alabama, Mississippi, and Nebraska—one is not yet treated as an adult at age 18. Before the pandemic, three states—Arizona, Florida, and Nevada—allowed remote witnessing of Wills. State law changes made in response to the need for social distancing during the current worldwide health crisis are rapidly adding to this number, and to the number of states with statutes allowing electronic Wills. Statutes vary as to the effect of divorce on estate planning documents. There is enormous variation, state to state, in the cost of probate and the fees allowed to PRs and lawyers administering estates.

By the time this book comes out, numerous statements made in this book may have been superseded. It's a tricky business, trying to corral the laws of fifty states and the District of Columbia.

All of which is to say that, if you want your estate plan to work, it is critically important that you consult regularly with a Trusts and Estates lawyer licensed in your state. It is that person's job to keep up with changes in the law and to understand how they apply to your facts.

With the knowledge you have gained from this book, you are positioned to understand and maintain an estate plan that will accomplish your goals.

APPENDIX
A

HELPFUL WEBSITES

FINDING A QUALIFIED ESTATE PLANNING ATTORNEY

www.actec.org

Use this site to find a Fellow of the American College of Trust and Estate Counsel (ACTEC) near you. If there is no Fellow within a reasonable distance of your zip code, contact another Fellow in your state to get a recommendation for an attorney near you. Fellows are often aware of good non-ACTEC Trust and Estate lawyers who happen to practice in other parts of their state.

INTESTATE DISTRIBUTIONS

www.mystatewill.com

This site, maintained by a private attorney, has a surprising amount of information about intestate distribution statutes, including about the numerous variations that may occur state to state.

ARRANGEMENTS FOR PETS

American Society for the Prevention of Cruelty to Animals
www.aspca.org ("pet trust")

This site helps with making arrangements for care of pets when you are gone. It lists the "pet trust" statutes in all 50 states and the District of Columbia.

DIVISION OF TANGIBLE PERSONAL PROPERTY

www.yellowpieplate.umn.edu

This site, from the University of Minnesota, has a wealth of suggestions to help in the disposition of tangible personal property. TPP raises some thorny questions in families when the patriarch or matriarch dies and distribution is being made to the next generation. The site sells a book and other resources to guide a family through these issues, but also has a good bit of helpful information free of charge.

ADVANCE DIRECTIVES

AARP
www.aarp.org (check "care of family," "end of life")

Aging with Dignity
www.agingwithdignity.org (Five Wishes form used in 42 states)

National Hospice and Palliative Care Organization
www.caringinfo.org/state (advance-directive forms)

U.S. Living Will Registry
www.uslivingwillregistry.com

Center for Practical Bioethics
www.midbio.org/mbc-cc.htm

POLST

See www.polst.org/map for information about the provisions
for medical orders pertaining to sustaining treatment.

RIGHTS AND OBLIGATIONS WITH RESPECT TO FUNERALS

Federal Trade Commission
www.ftc.gov (type in "funerals")

This site has many practical suggestions, including shopping
in advance of need, to avoid pressure. The site also discusses
the rights of consumers and obligations of funeral homes.

Funeral Consumer Alliance
www.funerals.org.

This site provides help from the industry.

SECTION 529 PLANS

www.savingforcollege.com

This site has a great deal of useful information, including information about specific states' programs, how the law underlying Section 529 plans operates, and more.

CAREGIVERS

General information:
National Academy of Elder Law Attorneys
naela.com

American Bar Association Commission on Law and Aging
abanet.org/aging

Support for those giving care
　　Family Caregiver Alliance
caregiver.org
　　National Alliance for Caregiving
caregiving.org

CAREGIVER CONTRACTS

www.aplaceformom.com

This site lists elements that should be considered when contracting with a caregiver and provides a form of contract.

www.care.com

This site has a simple contract available for use.

FINDING UNCLAIMED PROPERTY

Bank and brokerage accounts:

Unclaimed.org—follow links to the applicable states

In 2018, the District of Columbia returned more than $20 million to almost 19,000 claimants through its unclaimed property site.

Pensions:

Askebsa.dol.gov/abandonedplansearch (401(k))

This site searches on the basis of the name of the plan or the name of the Qualified Termination Administrator (QTA).

Pbgc.gov/search-unclaimed-pensions (pension plans)

This site, operated by the Pension Benefit Guarantee Corporation (established under the Employee Retirement Income Security Act of 1974), states that more than $300 million of pension assets are waiting to be claimed. The potential claimants are owed anywhere from 12 cents to almost $1 million. The six states with the most unpaid pension moneys outstanding are California, Illinois, New Jersey, New York, Ohio, and Texas.

INFORMATION TO COMPILE
FOR LOVED ONES

FOR WHILE YOU ARE ALIVE

Information that would be helpful or necessary for the agent on your advance medical directive or health care Power of Attorney is the following:

- Your legal name, address, date of birth

- Other names by which you are regularly known

- Mobile telephone number, email address

- Social Security Number

- Preferred hospital

- Health-insurance company and patient number, contact information

- Medicare number

- Primary doctor's name and contact information

- Same for specialists you see regularly

- Blood type

- Allergies to medications, and other allergies

- Whether you have a pacemaker, or other such device, with model number

- Copy of advance medical directive or health care Power of Attorney

- Medications used, dosages, and purposes

- Contact information for close family and friends.

FOR WHEN YOU DIE

It is hard to overestimate the amount of information your Personal Representative will need in order to administer and distribute your estate. The Office of Gift Planning at

Georgetown University in Washington, DC, has published a 23-page book with blank spaces to help one assemble this information. Information about your birth, marriage(s), children, career, assets, liabilities, location of documents, professionals' contact information, wishes for funeral and disposition of your body are all needed or useful when the time comes.

Below is an *abbreviated* list of information that your family or other fiduciaries will need when you die. Supplement as needed.

Legal papers:

- Birth certificate

- Marriage/divorce papers

- Citizenship papers

- Adoption papers

- Orders for Legal Name changes

- Military-discharge papers

- Funeral home contracts

Financial documents:

- Bank/brokerage account numbers and location

- Insurance policies insuring you or owned by you on the life of others

- Loan documents

- Beneficiary designations for retirement benefits and insurance products

- Credit-card information

- Social Security information

Copies of:

- Will

- Revocable Trust

- Any other trust documents

- Beneficiary designation forms

- Latest income-tax return

- (Also, *location* of original, ink-signed documents)

CONTACT INFORMATION FOR:

- Lawyer

- Accountant

- Financial Adviser

- Bank and trust-company contacts

- Family members and heirs, whether or not they are named as beneficiaries in your estate plan

- Beneficiaries and fiduciaries of estate plan

OTHER:

- Outline of wishes for funeral

- Car title

- Copy of driver's license, passport, credit cards

- Document showing desired distribution of tangible personal property

- Description of where to find current passwords for digital accounts

ABOUT THE AUTHOR

Virginia A. ("Ginny") McArthur practiced trusts and estates law in the District of Columbia, Maryland and Virginia for more than 35 years. In 2015 she retired from the law firm she established in 1992, McArthur Franklin, PLLC, which continues today as Franklin, Karibjanian &  Law, PLLC. She is a Retired Fellow of the American College of Trust and Estate Counsel (ACTEC), a former President of the Washington, DC Estate Planning Council, and former chair of the steering committee of the DC Bar's Section on Estates, Trusts and Probate Law. For 20 years Ginny co-authored the regularly updated volume for lawyers: *Wills, Trusts and Estates for the D.C. Area Practitioner* (LexisNexis Matthew Bender). She lives in Washington, DC, with her husband, Michael Higgins.

ABOUT THE AUTHOR